PUFFIN BOOKS
Editor: Kaye Webb

PILGRIMS OF THE WILD

Grey Owl, or Wa-Sha-Quon-Asin, as he was named by the tribe of Canadian Indians which adopted him, was born in Hastings, though for a large part of his life he was a successful guide and trapper in the Canadian backwoods. When he returned to his hunting grounds at the end of the First World War he found that the get-rich-quick trappers had driven the wildlife northwards and resolved to follow them. It was one winter when he and his companion Anahareo, the daughter of an Iroquois chief, adopted two orphaned kitten beaver, that changed Grey Owl's way of life.

Living with the beavers at such close quarters and worrying that the wild life in the Canadian forests was rapidly disappearing and in some areas was almost extinct, particularly the beavers, Grey Owl gave up trapping altogether and instead began to work for the preservation and conservation of the wilderness, and the beavers in particular.

When ecology and preservation are so much in everyone's thoughts today, it is intriguing to think that nearly fifty years ago Grey Owl had the vision and foresight to realize what was happening, and the determination to do something practical about it, although he and Anahareo almost starved in the attempt. So successful was he, finally, that the Canadian government appointed him official protector of the beavers under the National Parks of Canada.

Pilgrims of the Wild is Grey Owl's own story of his fascinating and exciting life, and the lives of Jelly Roll, Rawhide, McGinty and McGinnis, and the many other lovable and memorable members of his beaver family.

Grey Owl

PILGRIMS OF THE WILD

Abridged by Olive Jones
with a Foreword by Lovat Dickson

PUFFIN BOOKS

Puffin Books: a Division of Penguin Books Ltd,
Harmondsworth, Middlesex, England
Penguin Books Australia Ltd, Ringwood, Victoria, Australia

—

First published 1935
Abridged edition published in Puffin Books 1973

—

Made and printed in Great Britain
by C. Nicholls & Company Ltd
Set in Linotype Pilgrim

Dedicated to my friend and adviser

J. C. CAMPBELL

whose vision and sympathy and understanding
alone made possible the fulfilment of a
long-cherished purpose

Contents

Illustrations

Preface for Puffin Edition of
Pilgrims of the Wild

WHEN this book was published, and, in fact, until his death in 1938, Grey Owl was believed to have been a Métis, that is a man of mixed North American Indian and white blood. But then it was revealed that he had come to Canada from England as a young man of seventeen, and although a certain degree of mystery surrounded his parents' lives, there was no question but that his father was an Englishman named George Belaney, and his mother an American girl whose name had been Kitty Morris, and that he had been born in the respectable seaside town of Hastings on 16 September 1888, six weeks after his parents arrived there from America.

George's widowed mother, Mrs Belaney, and her two daughters, Caroline and Adelaide, lived in Hastings. When his parents departed almost as suddenly as they had arrived, these three ladies took over the upbringing of the little boy who had been christened Archibald Stansfeld Belaney.

From his earliest childhood on he was mad about Indians. The books he read were nearly all on this subject. Buffalo Bill's Wild West Show was touring England at the time, and all boys played Scouts and Indians. But that meant chiefly 'scalping' forays, alarming the woods with blood-curdling screeches, and crashing through the undergrowth. Young Archie's games were different, and they were solitary. He went tracking in the woods, learnt to 'freeze' near animals and study their behaviour. He trained himself to endure hardship, go for long periods without food, and sleep on the bare ground. In 1906, soon after leaving Hastings Grammar School, he made his way to Northern Ontario.

Within a year he had learnt how to be a trapper. He married an Ojibway girl of the isolated Bear Island Band at Temagami, and she and some of the old Indians among her people, taught him not only their language, for they could speak little English themselves, but how to survive in the bush, where winter and summer both carry dangers for the tenderfoot. They also taught him the myths and tales that are passed from one generation of the Indians to the next. He had not yet begun to write, but the instincts of the writer were already there, and in his imagination he stored up a romantic picture of these people, as changeless as the face of the remote wilderness they lived in. He grew his hair long, wore buckskin clothes and moccasins made for him by his wife from the skins of animals they had hunted. He was eventually adopted by the Ojibways, and given the name of Wa-Sha-Quon-Asin, which means He Who Flies By Night, whence Grey Owl. And soon, except for his blue eyes, he appeared a typical Indian of the northern bush, earning his living by trapping in the winter and guiding in the summer.

Grey Owl served in the First World War as a sniper with a Canadian battalion. He was wounded and gassed. When he returned to his own hunting grounds in 1918, it was to find them ravaged by get-rich-quick trappers, and men evading military service who had taken to the woods. They had used strychnine as bait, and dynamite to blow up beaver houses. They had been careless in setting fires so that great stretches of the bush had been burnt out. The animals had retreated towards the north, the *terre haute* as it is called, the Height of Land. Grey Owl found his livelihood threatened by the lack of game, and it was then that he began the pilgrimage you are going to read about in this book.

With him was Anahareo, the beautiful young Iroquois girl. The journey begun then was to cover two thousand miles and take two years. In the end, as you will read, the hunter and the hunted lay down together in peace, and Grey Owl swore never to kill another beaver.

How this happened, how they rescued two little beaver kittens, as the young are called, whose mother had been drowned in one of his traps, and how the kittens conquered them, and how they started a beaver colony, makes one of the great animal stories of the world. This action was also far-reaching in its consequences. Brought to the verge of starvation by his vow not to take another animal life for profit, Grey Owl started to write to pay the grocery bill. His articles were published in English and Canadian magazines, and they caught the attention of the world. The Canadian Government was forced to act. It offered Grey Owl a safe refuge for his beavers at Lake Ajawaan in Saskatchewan, and the Government, in conjunction with the provinces of Canada, instituted a close season for beaver trapping. Before he died, Grey Owl was to see the beaver houses filling up again.

He wrote four books in the next ten years, *Men of the Last Frontier*, *Pilgrims of the Wild*, *The Adventures of Sajo*, and *Tales of an Empty Cabin*. He came to England and appeared on lecture platforms; many thousands of people heard him. At the end of his visit he was invited to Buckingham Palace, and gave a lecture and showed his pictures to the Royal Family. On his return to Canada the

Prime Minister entertained him at dinner. A few weeks later, worn out by the exertions of his tour, he died of pneumonia on 13 April 1938. His body is buried at Ajawaa, and his cabin there is now being restored by the Canadian Government as a monument to his memory.

What has made his story live? Ever since European men first encountered the North American Indian, they have been fascinated by some mystic quality he possesses, which the European himself is conscious of having lost. 'When the wind speaks to the leaves, the Indian hears and understands', Grey Owl wrote.

This is what you will hear in his books, the voice of Nature speaking, the wild frenzy of hurrying rapids, the sound of whistling masses of snow being whirled across the winter lakes, the squeal of toboggan runners on ice. In that sound-world quite different from the one we are used to in towns and cities, you will hear the animals communicating with one another over the whole range of emotions, rage, sorrow, fear, joy. . . . It is as though one had stepped on to another planet, inhabited by a race of people never before encountered. It is the great charm of Grey Owl's books that in them he leads us back to that primitive world which our far-off ancestors knew, but from which the generations of men deafened by the din of technology have been exiled.

Toronto,   LOVAT DICKSON
Canada,
June 1972

Preface

THIS is primarily an animal story; it is also the story of
two people, and their struggle to emerge from the chaos
into which the failure of the fur trade, and the breaking
down of the old proprietary system of hunting grounds,
plunged the Indian people, and not a few whites, during
the last two decades. Their means of livelihood destroyed
by fire and the invasion by hordes of transient trappers and
cheap fur buyers, these two, a man and woman, with no
prospects, broke loose from their surroundings, taking with
them all that was left to them of the once vast heritage of
their people: their equipment and two small animals as
pets.

Outcasts in their own country, wandering in what
amounted to a foreign land, they tried desperately to fit
somewhere into this new picture. Their devotion to these
creatures that represented to them the very soul of their
lost environment, eventually proved to be their salvation.

All the places are actual, the story known to not a few;
characters are real, and if named receive, save in one instance, their proper appellations.

In order to grasp properly the spirit in which this book
is written, it is necessary to remember that though it is not
altogether an Indian story, it has Indian background. The
considering attitude towards all nature which appears
throughout the work, is best explained by a quotation
from John G. Gifford's 'Story of the Seminole War'.

'The meaning of sovereignty is not very clear to primitive peoples, especially to the Indian. He rarely dominated the things around him; he was a part of nature and not its boss.' Hewitt says of the Indian:

'In his own country ... he is a harmonious element in a landscape that is incomparable in its nobility of colour and mass and feeling of the Unchangeable. He never dominates it as does the European his environment, but belongs there as do the mesas, skies, sunshine, spaces and the other living creatures. He takes his part in it with the clouds, winds, rocks, plants, birds and beasts, with drum beat and chant and symbolic gesture, keeping time with the seasons, moving in orderly procession with nature, *holding to the unity of life in all things*, seeking no superior place for himself but merely a state of harmony with all created things ... the most rhythmic life ... that is lived among the races of men.' This viewpoint is not peculiar to people of native blood but is often found in those of other races who have resided for many years in the wilderness.

The idea of domination and submission, though now passing out of date in nearly every walk of life, is hard to disassociate, in the minds of some, from the contact between civilized man and beings in a state of nature. This was forcibly illustrated in a late radio broadcast during which, in a play dealing with frontier conditions, an actor who portrayed the part of Indian guide was heard to address the head (not the leader, as is generally supposed, the guide being of necessity in that capacity) of the party, in an awed voice, as 'Master'. But the more tolerant and unaspiring, though perhaps less ambitious view-point of the Indian must be taken into consideration, if the reader is to fully appreciate the rather unusual tenor of the narrative.

Interpretations of the more obscure mental processes of

the animal characters that run through the story, are of necessity comparative; such attempts at delineation are difficult, and often inadequate, without some parallel to draw them by; but the great majority of the descriptions of animal psychology are very clear and positive. Those manifestations that were at the time inexplicable have been construed in the light of later investigation and experience, so as to preserve the unity of impression of the narrative.

In the rather ill-considered rush we have been in to exploit our natural resources, we have taken little trouble to examine into the capabilities and possibilities of the wild creatures involved in it, save in so far as the findings were of commercial value. Therefore much that is interesting has been overlooked. The kinship between the human race and the rest of our natural fauna becomes very apparent to those of us who sojourn among the latter for any length of time; alarmingly so to those whose attitude has hitherto been governed by the well-worn and much abused phrase that 'Man shall have dominion over all'. However I do not draw comparisons between man and beast, save in a few instances which are too remarkable to be overlooked. Nor do I ascribe human attributes to animals. If any of their qualities are found to closely approximate some of our own, it is because they have, unknown to us, always possessed them, and the fault lies in our not having discovered sooner that these characteristics were not after all exclusively human, any more than are a number of others to which we have by long usage become accustomed.

My fingers, well toasted at many an open fire, and stiffened a little by the paddle and the pull of a loaded toboggan, are ill suited for the task I set them to. In this writing game I find myself in the dangerous situation of a man who has played his first game of poker and won a small jackpot, and who is now sitting in on another round having rather disastrous possibilities. To each his craft and calling, nor should we grudge another his ability; none the less, did I have the power to expertly carry out what I have here attempted, or had another, more skilled in letters and who knew this story well, have undertaken it, it would have been better done.

To me the rifle has ever been mightier than the pen. The feel of a canoe gunnell at the thigh, the splash of flying spray in the face, the rhythm of the snowshoe trail, the beckoning of far-off hills and valleys, the majesty of the tempest, the calm and silent presence of the trees that seem to muse and ponder in their silence; the trust and confidence of small living creatures, the company of simple men; these have been my inspiration and my guide. Without them I am nothing. To these and to my teachers, men of a type that is rapidly passing from the face of the earth, belongs the credit for whatever there may be that is worthy in this work of mine.

And should any part of it provide an hour of pleasure to just a few of those who love the Great Outdoors, or who have a kindly thought for a simple people or for a lowly animal, or should I perchance touch somewhere a chord of sympathy, or make some slight appeal to the sense of fair play of any of those true Sportsmen to whom Wild Life owes so much today, I will count my work, with all its imperfections, as having been worth while.

Wa-Sha-Quon-Asin (Grey Owl)

BEAVER LODGE,
PRINCE ALBERT NATIONAL PARK,
SASKATCHEWAN
7 November 1933

BOOK ONE

TOULADI

Prologue

OUTSIDE a window from which the sash has been removed stands a man, alert, silent, watchful.

The cabin beside which he keeps post faces out on to a
lake, its frontage at the water's edge. The slopes of the surrounding hills are covered with a heavy forest, the tall
grey poplars and giant spruce standing close in a dark and
serried palisade about the camp. The water is calm and un-
ruffled; the lake appears to sleep. There is no sound and no
movement save the desultory journeyings of a squirrel, engaged in salvaging cones he has been dropping from the
spruce tops.

In front of the man, and directed through the aperture
into the building, is a motion picture camera, trained on
the door, which is closed. The interior of the building is
equipped with the rude but comfortable furnishings and
the simple utensils of a woodsman's home, for the greater
part of the dwelling is given over to human occupancy,
and is a permanent abode, although it has one peculiarity.
Across one end of it is a large erection having the appearance of a massive earthwork, shoulder high and occupying
easily one-third of the floor space.

Outside, in strategic positions commanding the door
and the approach from the lake, are other men, holding
cameras. Inside the building a man sits in a chair, waiting.

Suddenly, 'All right! here he comes,' cries a watcher.
The man at the window stands poised, ready. There can

now be heard, approaching the entrance, a heavy measured tread. The camera commences to whir and simultaneously with a resounding thump the door is thrown widely open and there steps over the threshold a full-grown beaver, erect, and bearing in his arms a load of earth and sticks.

Walking upright like a man, steadily, purposefully, looking neither to the right nor to the left, past the stove, round the table, between the benches, he pursues his undeviating way towards the earthwork. The camera swings, follows him, grinding. But for that sound and the thudding of the beaver's heavy steps, there is silence. Straight up the side of the lodge, for such the earthwork is, the beaver marches, deposits his load, tamps it in with his hands; he pushes in a stick to bind it, cuts off the protruding end and potters at some small repairs. At this moment another larger beaver enters hauling a six foot stick which she skilfully manoeuvres through the opening, drawing it over to the house and up the side of it. The two animals work with the heavy pole, placing it; they are very particular and take some time at this. Meanwhile the man in the chair rises, shuts the door and resumes his seat.

The camera drones on.

Another beaver, small, brisk, business-like, emerges from a hole in the side of the lodge, places two sticks very carefully, looks around, becomes fidgety and scampers in again. The operator's face is a study; he is getting it all. Yesterday he got a moose passing through the door yard, the day before a group of muskrats.

The two big beavers at last finish their job to their complete satisfaction; and now their purposeful, sober mien deserts them. On all fours and at a little trot, they run over to the seated man and stand erect beside him, looking up at him. Their inquiring faces reach waist high on him as he sits. They must weigh one hundred pounds between the two of them. The larger one, the female, plucks at his sleeve trying to attract his attention. The camera grinds steadily and the beavers undoubtedly hear it. But they pay no heed; this is their fourth year at the business.

The man strokes the animals' heads.

'Well! how is it going today, old-timers?' he asks.

A series of short, sharp, ejaculations from the larger one as she pulls impatiently at his hand with her forepaws.

'All right, here's your apple,' says the man, and seizing the offering, she runs, hops, and trots over to the door, opens it inwards, with a quick pull at a leather loop, and runs outside. The other, her consort, patient, more sedate, gently takes his apple, and slips quietly out.

The camera at the window stops. Outside other machines click, for down at the waterfront, a scant thirty feet away, are more beavers, swimming, playing, eating.

All at once one of them stands upright, sniffing the air, listening, a stiff brown pillar of attention; a foreign scent has drifted down from that dark unknown forest with its threat of a thousand dangers. Without warning the beaver leaps into the water with a terrific plunge, slaps his tail. Immediately there is a violent commotion, cries, splashes, heavy thudding of broad flat tails, and in a moment not a beaver is to be seen.

Silence falls, the water quickly subsides. There is nothing visible, though the machines are cocked and ready. But their work is finished. They will get nothing more today.

It has all been very casual, in a way. No rehearsing has been done, no commands given; the actors have done just about as they liked. The beavers are free and unrestrained and could be gone beyond all hope of recovery in an hour. But they prefer to stay here, and year by year have made this place their home, have even built their domicile within the human habitation, a subterranean passage leading from it to the bottom of the lake.

Extraordinary behaviour for an animal supposed to be wild and unapproachable! Perhaps it is. But the story that lies behind this little scene is even stranger. It is not a tale of heroism, or hazard, or very high accomplishment, but has more to tell of loyalty and tolerance, and of the bond between a woman and a man. There is much joy in it, a little sorrow, some loneliness and struggle, and some rare good fun. I know that story very well, and how it all began.

I

How Anahareo had her way

THE town of Bisco was dropping fast astern as I dipped and swung my paddle, driving my light, fast canoe steadily northward to the Height of Land. It was not much of a town as towns go. It had no sidewalks, and no roads, and consisted mainly of a Hudson's Bay store, a saw mill, probably fifty houses scattered on a rocky hillside, and an Indian encampment in a sheltered bay of Biscotasing Lake, on the shores of which this village stood. But it was rather a noted little place, as, being situated within measurable distance of the headwaters of a number of turbulent rivers such as the Spanish, the White, the Mississauga, the Mattawgami, the Ground-hog and others, and being moreover the gateway to a maze of water routes that stretch southward to lakes Huron and Superior, and northward to the Arctic ocean, the fame of its canoemen was widely known. That part of the District of Algoma, in the Province of Ontario, had until lately been one of the best furproducing territories in Northern Canada, but an influx of get-rich-quick transient hunters had depleted the furbearing animals almost to the point of extinction, and times were not what they had been.

Reduced though it might be, none the less this isolated post had been my home town for the fifteen years since I had drifted down from the north, if coming out to sell fur and replenish supplies twice a year can be said to establish citizenship. I had seen my best years in the vast forest and on the intricate waterways that commenced at its back door and stretched many hundreds of miles into the interior, and was leaving behind me friendships with both red men and white, that had been cemented by year after year of trial by ordeal in the crucible of hardship; and I was feeling a little choked up and lonely.

The farewell celebrations had been a little lively, and I was not the only one leaving town that evening, but the others were all headed in the opposite direction, to their stamping grounds on the distant Mississauga whose pine-crowned cliffs, maple crested ridges, and wild fierce rapids I might never see again. So I thought as I plugged along, the little swirling eddies that slid from my paddle singing a low whispering dirge in the silence of that spring night.

Less than a dozen miles brought me to the first portage. Certain hints dropped by the Hudson's Bay Manager who was also Chief of Police (he was, in fact, the whole force) made it seem advisable to cross this immediately. It was four miles long and I had two loads, outfit and canoe. But the footing was good and there was a moon. In the ensuing labour a lot of my depression of spirits oozed through my pores in the form of perspiration. It was an arduous trip, eight miles loaded and four empty on the middle return journey; but it was completed soon after sunrise when I made camp, slept till noon, and then proceeded on my pilgrimage.

A disastrous bush fire had swept my hunting ground, leaving it a barren area of cracked rock, burnt out stumps and tortured tree trunks, and I was bound north and east to the far off, supposedly fruitful ranges of the Abitibi district in Northern Quebec; a vast country which, so rumour had it, was little explored and was populated only by a few wandering bands of Ojibway[1] Indians. Much of my route

1. Pronounced O-*jib*-way, accented on the second syllable.

24

lay through a country I had known. It was now almost un-recognizable. A railroad had been built through part of it. There were huge burns, areas of bare rocks and twisted rampikes, miles of staring desolation. Riff-raff bushmen, dirty, unkempt; stolid European peasantry tearing down the forest; settlers on stone farms (two crops a year – one snow and the other rocks) existing, no more. The change was nearly unbelievable. Immured in the fastness of the Mississauga I had not known what had been going on. I passed on uneasy, fearful, wondering what lay ahead. There was plenty!

Old Fort Mattawgami, the river dammed, was flooded out, all under water save the little Mission Church which stood awash on a knoll. I had a noon meal on its steps, sorrowfully. Another trading post, a startling new pale-looking affair, stood on the far shore on high land.

I met some old-time faces, men who had made history in these parts; I got the news such as it was. It sounded to me more like a Book of Doom. Flying Post was on its last legs, its Indians dispersed. Ancient John Buffalo on the Montreal River, a trapper of the old régime, almost a land-mark in the country, dead these many years. Snape, who ran Moose Factory at a time when a round trip from the front took six weeks fast voyaging, now manager of a Hud-son's Bay Company store in a small town, his ankle broken and badly knit – off the trail for keeps. Andy Luke, who habitually carried 400 lb on a portage and who had made big hunts that were a byword in the land, *working on the railroad as a labourer*; his son Sam, lean, wiry Sam with the speed and endurance of a greyhound, a wizard in a canoe, doing odd jobs. Tommy Saville, the White Indian, adopted by the Ojibways when young and who had made and spent a fortune in a gold rush, living in a house in a town, eating his heart out for the trail, sneaking down cellar to boil a pail of tea over a little fire of shavings – to get the feel of it again.

What did it all mean; was the whole Wilderness falling about our ears?

I kept going. Further on the tale improved but little. Shining Tree and Gowganda, rich camps of earlier days, were still kept alive by many of the old originals, waiting for a break, hoping with the perennial optimism of the dyed-in-the-wool prospector, for a new strike to keep the old camp going. The whole Gowganda lake area had been burnt to the bare rock.

I encountered Indians, white woodsmen, real prospectors, each meeting an experience. But when their conversation turned to future plans there were evidences of a vague foreboding in their speech. No man felt secure. Fire, railroads, power projects, the aeroplane, they were tearing the old life apart. The Frontier was rolling back like a receding tide. I must hurry.

Four hundred miles' travel brought me to a town on the Temiskaming and Northern Ontario Railway which, when I first saw it, had been a frontier post. Before the coming of the steel, rare sportsmen and adventurers, seeking the freedom and spiritual satisfaction to be found in an untouched virgin territory, had come here at intervals. We guided them, a strange, new, interesting job; these men had been our comrades on the trail. We talked about such a trip all winter, and showed each other the letters we got from our patrons. The place was now a populous tourist resort. An automobile highway was in the making. I took a job here; the party was a good one, people from New York, with all the genial good fellowship of the American on a vacation. But there was a false note. Guides were no longer companions, they were lackeys, footmen, toadies; a kind of below-stairs snobbery had sprung up among them – kid-glove guiding; some of them actually wore white cotton gloves at their work. Old-timers talked about it, shook their heads – but they had to follow suit; fur was gone and this now emasculated occupation was their only means of subsistence.

My main outfit had been sent around to this place by freight; I shipped it ahead three hundred miles, replenished my supplies and left, in my heart rebellion and disillusionment. This place held memories I had hoped to renew. I pitied the pine trees standing there. They had to stay.

I had billed my freight to a point on the Transcontinental where I arrived a month later, renewed my food supply and sent the outfit another stage ahead. In this manner, touching the railroad at strategic points, a journey was made that covered approximately two thousand miles. This occupied two years, during which time I wandered on in the summer time, and trapped with more or less success wherever Fall caught me.

The waters began to go crossways of my projected line of travel rather than with it, necessitating an inordinate amount of portaging; so that the last leg of the journey was made ignominiously on a train, with the outfit in the baggage car, out of which the canoe regarded me reproachfully at every stop. There was, however, another very compelling reason for this dereliction; my correspondence, usually nonexistent, now demanded constant attention. At a summer resort where I had guided for a short time the year before, there had been a girl, a cultured, talented and personable young woman of the Iroquois, a cut or two above me perhaps, but not, I hoped, on that account unattainable. The affair was quite wanting in the vicissitudes and the harrowing but stirring episodes that are said usually to beset the path of high romance. The course of true love ran exasperatingly smooth; I sent the lady a railroad ticket, she came up on a pullman and we were married, precisely according to plan. The complications started afterwards.

In order that the blame will not attach in the wrong places, I must here give a brief outline of two very conflicting personalities. We were, in many ways, exact opposites. In my young days I had received some pretty intensive home tuition from an ever-blessed aunt, but had shown little aptitude save in geography, history and English. In the latter subject the ground work had been solid, and as I now see, very skilfully laid. But I had so far taken no trouble to build on it. Most of my time from middle youth on had been spent in solitude or largely amongst a people whose language was not English, and confused by regional dialects. Only a retentive memory and a passion for reading had kept alive this early training, and my precise and somewhat stilted English was, like a stiff and ceremonious suit of Sunday best, something to be taken out of the closet and worn on occasion, and its use ended, returned to the limbo of unneeded things. I was careless in my speech and quickly resented any infringement on what I considered to be my personal freedom. This last trait had been intensified by the discipline endured in the army. I had been one of those unusual people, so seldom met with in stories, who entered the army as a private and left it as one. I had come back to the woods with my efficiency much impaired, and my outlook on things generally had been in no way improved by the job of sniper that I had held, and the sole educational effect the war had been to convince me of the utter futility of civilization. Most of my views, whilst free and unconventional were correspondingly narrow.

My wife Anahareo was not highly educated, save in that broader sense which is not always the result of schooling.

She had a passion for advancement, uplift, and a proper use of words and took a lively interest in world events. She was a direct descendant of hereditary Iroquois chiefs, and her father was one of the original Mohawk river-men who had helped to make history along the Ottawa in the days of the great square-timber rafts; she came of a proud race. She was strictly modern, as modern went at that time, a good dancer and conversationalist, and, a particular dresser herself, she naturally wanted me always to look my best. My idea of looking my best was to wear my hair long, have plenty of fringes on my buckskins, to allow one tassel of my Hudson Bay sash to hang behind like a tail, and to have the front of my shirt decorated with an oblique row of safety pins on each side, as a Cossack wears his ammunition, to be intriguingly glimpsed at times beneath a leather vest. These things were very dear to me, and as to the safety pins, why, they were real handy and served a useful as well as an ornamental purpose, being used to hang up my clothes to dry at night. Other peculiarities born of long habit, and hitherto unnoticed, now became very obvious. I could not, or would not, carry on any conversation at all while in a canoe, and preferred to walk in single file, trail fashion as, like most bush people, I continually bumped into anyone who walked beside me; as a concession the lady was, in this case, always allowed to walk in front. These features were brought to my attention one by one, and it is easily seen that our honeymoon, spent with a load of supplies on the way into a hunting ground, must have been unusual and interesting.

I speedily discovered that I was married to no butterfly, that my companion could swing an axe, put up a tent in good shape, make quick fire, and could rig a tump-line[1]

1. A tump-line is a broad band round the head from which a load on the back is suspended.

and get a load across in good time, even if she did have to sit down and powder her nose at the other end of the portage. She habitually wore breeches, a custom not at that time so universal amongst women as it is now, and one that I did not in those days look on with any great approval. The apparel of our own women ran heavily to voluminous plaid skirts and gay tartan head shawls. This one wore top boots and a mackinaw shirt, and somehow achieved an appearance of rough and ready competence. While she was not very much of an expert at out-door cooking, I soon found that I had procured me a really first-class needle-woman.

She had brought up with her, as a dowry, a large pack-sack well stuffed with clothes, an ominous-looking volume entitled *The Power of Will*, five small tattered booklets comprising *The Irving Writing System*, under the mistaken impression that they were *Hints for Housewives*, and an exceedingly good felt hat which I gained possession of and still wear on special occasions.

The literary booklets were an oversight and belonged to her sister, and we had considered sending them back, though we never did; which, it afterwards turned out, was just as well.

This new wife of mine must have been very lonely at times, though she never said so. Once she suggested that we have a radio. This made me vaguely uncomfortable. We all had an idea in those days that radio caused electrical disturbances that had a bad effect on the weather. So I tactfully sidestepped the idea and we viewed the sunset through the one window of our cabin for relaxation; at that, these sunsets were often pretty good to look at. Eating was lots of fun too. We arose before daylight and often travelled all night. Snowshoes and toboggan, or canoe, were cared for almost like they had been horses, while the little woman waited patiently, wishing it was time to eat. She was, she said, becoming jealous of the bush. There was one particular ridge that I visited often and spoke highly of (value about two hundred dollars) as it was the abode of a number of marten, and my frequent visits there occupied whatever spare time I had. For this spot she had a special hatred and I, in my blind stupidity, could not see the reason.

We ate, slept, and dreamed lines of traps, and in the evenings laid out trails and pored over maps, or made preparations for the next day's excursion. I was engrossed by my work and talked of little else. The stern discipline of the trail ruled also in the cabin. The trail was my religion, and like any other fanatic I tried to force my views on even the one I loved. Altogether there were the makings of a first class domestic tragedy.

But the exigencies of constant travel and the demands made by our manner of living, left little time for temperamental readjustments, and the hurry and drive of the Fall and early winter trapping occupied the full of our days, until one evening just before Christmas, I returned from a short trip to find my proud and gallant Anahareo in a dishevelled and disconsolate heap upon the bunk, with a tear-stained face and her eyes swollen and red from weeping. And then the whole thing came out, everything, piece by piece. At first I could not understand; everything had seemed to be going first class. I had been a most appreciative husband, not at all indifferent or unattentive as the real Indians often were. This woman had won my lasting respect and admiration with her courage in the face of unaccustomed hardships, and I had let her know it. But that, it was now revealed, was not at all what she wanted. Respect! The dead got that. Admiration! What was that! — You admired scenery. We lived, it appeared, with all the sociability of sleigh dogs: we ate our meals with the same relish we enjoyed throwing wood through a stove-door.

And I listened amazedly to this strange contradictory creature that could sleep out in the rain with a smile, and cry over a lack of ceremony at meal times.

There was more, much more. Trap lines, plans! plans! – plans to inflict torture and death and then to go out and boast of it! I was startled at this latter accusation, and a little indignant. I was trying my best to earn us a living; a man had to kill whatever way he could, and all he could; fur was getting low. But the truth peered out in a most unwelcome fashion from between the lines of this recital, and when it was done I marched out of the house to visit my pet ridge, hurt, bewildered, and not a little angry. I made a fire up there and sat and smoked and thought the matter over while I skinned a marten, and fought my battle out alone as Anahareo had done this many days. And all at once I saw myself as I was, saw clearly the selfishness that had been bred in me during a life of solitary wandering, and realized how narrow was the rut that I had got into. And I went down that mountain trail at a run, my dignity, my accursed self-assurance thrown to the winds, and arrived home with my snowshoes nearly smoking, hoping I was not too late. You guessed it; I was not.

And so the threatening clouds of disaster rolled clean away. We worked as hard as ever, but I left the job outside the home where it belonged and we took a pride in our little cabin and made ornaments for it, and talked of many things that we had never before had time even to mention. We found our necessary partings longer now, and in our travels, where our trails forked, the one who arrived at the crossing first, spelt out a foolish message for the other in the snow; and we were very happy, at last. And Anahareo became her old self once again. But I never did.

Anahareo from now on followed the trap trails regularly and we were boon companions. Although it was her first winter at this rather strenuous occupation, she soon became so adept that she was able to take her turn at breaking trail, took care of side lines herself, and was altogether a good deal more of an assistance than some men partners I have had. She was strong and hardy, but this did not prevent her from realizing more and more keenly the cruelties of her new profession. The sight of frozen twisted forms contorted in shapes of agony, and the spectacle of submissive despairful beasts being knocked senseless with an axe handle, and hung up in a noose to choke out any remaining spark of life while the set was being made ready for a fresh victim, moved her to deep compassion. Worse, to her mind, were the great numbers of harmless birds and squirrels caught accidentally and to no good purpose, and often still alive, some screaming, others wailing feebly in their torment. And strangely some of these animals seemed to sense her feeling, and on more than one occasion a doomed animal would look not towards me, to the death that was so near, but at her, staring as though in dumb hopeless appeal to her for the mercy it must have known that I would never give.

These things made her very unhappy, which was a mild surprise to me, as I had supposed that, being of full Indian blood, she would have at least as much apathy for the sufferings of these animals that were providing us with the means to live, as had I myself.

I had long ago invested the creatures of the forest with a personality. This was the inevitable result of a life spent wandering over the vast reaches of a still, silent land in which they were the only form of animate life, and sprang from early training and folklore. Yet this concession gained them no respite, and although I never killed needlessly and was as merciful as was possible under the circumstances, the urge of debts to be paid, money to spend, and prestige to be maintained, lent power to the axe handle and cunning to the hands that otherwise might have faltered on occasion. Always I had pitied, but had closed my mind to all thoughts of compassion save in retrospect.

But my point of view was slowly changing. Forced at last to stop and look around and take stock, obliged now to think of someone else besides myself, I saw many things that had hitherto escaped me in my remorseless striving for achievement. My surroundings began to have a different aspect. I began to have a faint distaste for my bloody occupation. This was resolutely quenched.

Even in those less enlightened days, at a time when I actually believed that radio was spoiling the hunt by affecting the climate, I was perhaps not without a certain sense of justice which, though not recognized as such at the time, evinced itself in strange ways. A primitive and imaginative ancestry had not been without its influence. There were certain precepts, amounting to superstitions, that were strictly adhered to at no matter what cost in time and trouble. No bear was killed without some portion of the carcass, generally the skull or shoulder bones, being hung up in a prominent place somewhere in his former range. The bodies of beavers were laid in supposedly comfortable positions and the hands, feet and tail, severed for convenience in skinning, were laid beside or on the body. Whenever possible the body, with these appendages securely tied to it, was committed to the water through a hole laboriously cut in the ice. Those eaten had the kneecaps, unusual adjuncts for an animal, removed and most religiously burnt. All these ceremonies are practised by semi-civilized, and even more advanced Indians over a wide area; and should anyone be tactless enough to inquire the reason why they do these things, the answer if any, will be, 'Ozaam tapskoche anicianabé, mahween – because they are so much like Indians.'

I had however other customs of my own invention, and kept rigidly two self-imposed rules. I would allow no sportsman I guided to photograph a wounded animal until it was dead, and any animal that should chance to be brought to camp alive, must be resuscitated and let go.

At the termination of the Winter trapping season we went out to sell our fur. Prices had fallen, and were going down every week or so. Although we did not realize it, the day of the trapper was almost done. The hunting ground we were working had been previously trapped over by a noted hunter the winter before, and between that and the low prices we only took fur to the value of about six hundred dollars; not a great sum in comparison to what I had been in the habit of making during these boom years. There would be little left over after the debt was settled and a summer's provisions purchased. So I decided on a spring hunt to replenish the exchequer, something that went a little against even my principles, as a hunt at that time of the year was looked on as both destructive and cruel by the better class of trapper. But there was a family of beavers remaining over from the organized slaughter of the year before, and like too many of my kind, I salved my conscience by saying that I may as well clean them out before someone else stepped in and took them.

Delayed over a week at the post by the late arrival of a buyer, we did not arrive back at our ground until the last of May. The hunt should have been over by now, and I was a little disturbed over the hardship I could not now avoid inflicting, as the young beavers were most certainly born by now, and would perish after the old ones were removed. This proved to be the case. While making a set at an old, renovated beaver house where I knew the female to be, I heard faintly the thin piping voices of kitten beavers. In apparent clumsiness, I allowed my paddle to drop with a rattle on the canoe gunnell with the intention of hiding the sound, but Anahareo had heard it and begged me to lift the trap, and allow the baby beavers to have their mother and live. I felt a momentary pang myself, as I had never before killed a beaver at this time on that account, but continued with my work. We needed the money.

The next morning I lifted the bodies of three drowned beavers. The mother was missing however, one trap being unaccounted for. I found where the chain had been broken, and dragged for the body unsuccessfully, later breaking the dam and partly draining the pond, but without avail. She would be the largest and most valuable, so I bemoaned my loss and forgot the life that had been destroyed for nothing, and the helpless kittens left to starve. After a whole day spent in a fruitless search, I removed all traps and equipment and proceeded to camp, having no intention whatever of returning; but the next day, after skinning and stretching the catch, for no reason at all I changed my mind. So inauspiciously do important events intrude themselves into our lives. I portaged back to the ruined pond that would never again be good for anything, and we paddled over to the old beaver house in an effort to discover if the female had succeeded in getting back there, but could find no indication either by sight or sound of her presence.

So we turned to go, finally and for good. As we were leaving I heard behind me a light splash, and looking back saw what appeared to be a muskrat lying on top of the water alongside the house. Determined to make this wasted day pay, I threw up my gun, and standing up in the canoe to get a better aim, prepared to shoot. At that distance a man could never miss, and my finger was about to press the trigger when the creature gave a low cry, and at the same instant I saw, right in my line of fire another, who gave out the same peculiar call. They gave voice again, and this time the sound was unmistakeable – they were young beavers! I lowered my gun and said, 'There are your kittens.'

'Let us save them,' cried Anahareo excitedly, and then in a lower voice, 'It is up to us, after what we've done.'

'Yes; we have to,' I answered. 'Let's take them home.' It seemed the only fitting thing to do.

This was not such an easy matter as the kittens were well able to take care of themselves in the water, being older than I had thought. By the exercise of considerable patience and ingenuity we eventually caught them, and dropped them aboard, two funny-looking furry creatures with little scaly tails and exaggerated hind feet, that weighed less than half a pound apiece, and that tramped sedately up and down the bottom of the canoe with that steady, persistent, purposeful walk that we were later to know so well. We looked at them in a kind of dumbfounded bewilderment, hardly knowing what to do with them.

2

How we undertook a new responsibility

AT the time we did not know what we were letting ourselves in for. Any preconceived ideas either of us had on the raising and handling of pets had to be radically changed. These were no cringing terrorstricken wild things with feral eyes that cowered fearfully in dark corners, but a pair of very wide awake, aggressive personalities, who fastened themselves on us as their protectors. They gave themselves completely into our hands, and proceeded to levy unceasing demands on our attention. They allowed us at no time to forget the responsibilities that we had incurred, and before long they had us trained to sleep with one eye open and one hand on the milk can.

Feeding them was a problem. They would not drink the diluted milk out of a dish, and having no feeding bottle we conceived the idea of loading a slim twig with the sweet milk out of the can, closing the beaver's mouth over it with our fingers, and pulling out the stick. Masticating this sticky mass kept them interested for long periods at a time, and they did not need much of it, so this scheme simplified matters considerably. They were very gentle, and they had a kind of naïve disarming friendliness of disposition that took it quite for granted that they belonged, and that we were well disposed towards them and would see them through.

After feeding times they desired to be picked up and

fondled and it was not long before they made this a regular habit, falling asleep in odd places such as the inside of an open shirt, half way up a sleeve, or draped around a person's neck. Should they be removed from these places they would immediately awaken and return in the most determined manner, and if placed in their box they awoke at once, and with piercing outcries demanded to be again taken up, grasping our hands and lifting themselves up by means of them. They soon got to know our voices, and would answer concertedly with loud exclamations when spoken to.

We allowed them to roam around the tent at will, and occasionally on their rambles they would become lost and parted. Their bold self-confidence would then quickly desert them, and they became lonely and would call frantically for help, and on being placed together they would throw themselves on their backs with wiggles and squeals of joy, and lie down together holding tightly on to each other's fur. Often as they lay sleeping we would speak to them for the fun of having them awaken and answer us, which they invariably did, in their shrill childish treble. Should this, however, occur too often they would become very impatient and express their annoyance in no uncertain terms. Their voices were really the most remarkable thing about them, much resembling the cries of a human infant, without the volume but with a greater variety of expression, and at all hours of the day and night there was liable to be some kind of a new sound issuing from the interior of the box. The best known and easiest to recognize of these was the loud, long and very insistent call for lunch, which chorus broke out about every two hours.

It was not long before our diminutive charges became attached to us, and we to them. Each had a special liking for one of us, and continued faithful to his choice. They lavished this affection on us in a number of curious ways, such as upsetting the box, as soon as they were big enough to do so, and rushing out at us as we passed, or creeping into our blankets at night and cuddling up to us. They would generally lie on our bodies, one on each of us, the favoured position being a rather inconvenient one across the throat. If alarmed while out and around, they would come gliding along belly to the ground, each to his chosen friend, and sit quietly as two mice until the supposed danger had passed.

They were continually escaping, and the first few times this happened we hunted for them high and low, feeling ourselves pretty smart to ferret out two such small objects from the underbrush. But our anxiety and subsequent gratification were both quite unnecessary, as we discovered that on hearing us in the brush they would run towards us of their own accord. On this account we became over-confident, and one morning, having failed to close the box before retiring, we awoke to find their chamber empty, and no sign of a beaver any place in the tent. A prolonged and wide search failed to locate the wanderers. We hunted all that day both by canoe and on land, and remained out all night. It seemed hard to believe that they would desert us like that, attached to us as they seemed to be. We felt a little hurt about it. Realizing at last that they had been gone over thirty hours, we gave up the search and went home to get some sleep, not a little sad – and there in the tent, all unconscious of the excitement of which they were the cause, sat the two deserters on the bed, soaking wet, and squeezing the water out of their coats on to the blankets.

After this experience we simply pitched our camp near any old lake, and with due regard for predatory birds and beasts, we let them come and go as they pleased. They would walk down to the lake with that methodical step of theirs, bathe, swim, and play in the reeds awhile and return, plodding solemnly up and down the water trail together, like two little old men out for a constitutional. They were good housekeepers too. By this time they were beyond the milk stage, and to supplement their natural diet we fed them once a day on porridge and each had his dish, which when empty, was pushed over to the side of the tent, and the instinct for stacking used material as far out of the way as possible caused them to try and rear the plates against the wall. This was not easy to do, but they persisted at it and very often succeeded.

At three months of age they ceased to be of any further trouble to us save for the daily feed of porridge, an insatiable and very active curiosity regarding the contents of provision bags and boxes, the frequent desire for petting that seemed to fill some great want in their lives, and the habit they had of coming into our beds, soaking wet, at all hours of the night.

They were scrupulously clean, were gentle and good natured, they gave out no odour whatever, and were altogether the best conducted pair of little people one could wish to live with. They were very self-effacing, and a good deal of the time were neither to be seen nor heard; but always there came moments, generally about sundown, when they seemed to feel the need of some attention, and getting to know of this we made a point of giving it to them. And they would give little bleats and play with our hands, nibble our finger tips and climb on us, so far as climbing was possible to them, with many absurd but genuine evidences of real affection. This desire to be made much of, the appeal in their voices, the habit they had of playing with a lock of hair, a button or a buckskin fringe, made them seem very childlike to us.

That Anahareo should become devoted to them is not at

all remarkable; but my own attitude towards them was something quite beyond my expectations, and was even likely to have a compromising effect on our chief means of livelihood – the beaver hunt. I wondered at times if it was quite manly to feel as I did towards these small beasts. But I was able to call to my rescue the recollection of an ugly pock-marked Indian, a huge, evil-appearing man I had always disliked, but who spent a whole day in the rain searching for a young beaver he had lost; and when he recovered it, he came home in the pouring rain in his shirt sleeves carrying the shivering little creature wrapped up in his coat. Yet another had shot a good lead-dog for killing a beaver he had kept for two years as a pet. Evidently the little devils had a way of working on a person's sympathies, and at the commencement I was a little sly and furtive about them when Anahareo was around. Their utter dependence on our good will claimed all of any chivalry we had. Their little sneezes and childish coughs, their little whimpers and small appealing noises of affection, their instant and pathetically eager response to any kindness, their tiny clinging hand-like forepaws, their sometimes impatiently stamping feet, and their little bursts of independence, all seemed to touch a chord of tenderness for the small and helpless that lies dormant in every human heart. Riotously happy for the most part, they were at odd times subject to fits of peevishness and irritation, during which they quarrelled and slapped at one another and at us, but these moods were of short duration and were, we found, the result of improper feeding, which was later to have more serious results. Their hands – one can call them nothing else – were nearly as effective as our own more perfect members would be, in the uses they were put to. They could pick up very small objects with them, manipulate sticks and stones, strike, push, and heave with them and they had a very firm grasp which it was difficult to disengage. When peeling a stick they used them both to twist the stem with supple wrist movements, while the teeth rapidly whittled off the succulent bark as it went by, much after the fashion of a lathe.

They were greedy little fellows and were constantly trying to steal from one another. These attempts however were never very serious, and seldom successful. They would allow us to approach and handle them freely while eating, without any complaint, but if we attempted to lay hold of their wooden sandwich they would let out a sharp ejaculation or two, and promptly turn their backs on us.

Should we be away up the lake for any length of time, we would, on our return, call them whilst yet some distance away, and they would come to meet the canoe, answering the call with long high-pitched cries, and on close approach would reach up to us with outstretched hands in eager expectancy, grasping our fingers and looking up at us and making the most uncommon sounds. For we always made it a practice to bring along little bits of sweet things we made for them, and they would lie in the water eating them with loud enjoyment and a very audible smacking of lips.

Towards the middle of summer it became necessary to go out to the railroad to confer with others of my calling on the possibilities of the coming winter. On this journey, while in the canoe, we let the beavers run loose as they were not able to climb out of it. On the portages they were dumped into a grain bag and dangled from a thwart of the inverted canoe. One of these carries was two miles in length, and they cried the whole way while mosquitoes settled on the bag in swarms. Having no longer a box, at camping grounds we hung them up in the bag near a fire to keep the mosquitoes from them, so they were at times

43

pretty well smoked. They slept nearly all the time and ate nothing, but arrived in fair shape except that they were a little groggy. An Indian who came to see them said they were dying, but an hour or two in the water restored them. It was now necessary to confine them both day and night, owing to the presence of a multitude of idle sleigh dogs that formed the larger part of the population of the village. They expressed their disapprobation of this treatment by promptly eating their way out of everything we tried to keep them in, so that they had me busy providing boxes which lasted, if they were good, one night.

Another trip had yet to be made to the trapping camp for some equipment that remained there, so we left the beavers in care of a friend who locked them carefully into an outhouse built of logs. We returned a few days later with our load, and as soon as we disembarked Anahareo went to visit the beavers, while I crossed immediately over to the store to obtain a good strong box, as we expected to board a train that evening. I was met on my way back by a pale and distraught Anahareo. . . . The beavers were gone! They had eaten through the timbers at the thin place where two logs rested one on the other, and gone on a tour. Our friend was greatly disturbed at their loss, knowing how we prized them. He muzzled a beaver dog, an animal especially trained to hunt them, and set out to trail them down. I commenced to comb the surrounding woods, covering the ground in the direction of the lake which was some considerable distance away. The beavers had not been gone long, and could, under ordinary circumstances, have been easily recovered; the danger was grave only on account of the huskies of which there were dozens, and cheap-skate hunters who would kill anything on sight.

We were not long away before one of the beavers, the female, showed up in the yard, picking her way non-

chalantly among several dogs, some of whom were commencing to circle warily behind her. With a shout and a
wild leap Anahareo threw herself between them, and grab-
bing up the startled beaver ran for the nearest door, pursued by the enemy. This I learned on my return from an
unsuccessful search. And when the hunting dog returned
and was found to have failed also,[1] we, Anahareo and I,
looked at one another silently and with one common
thought – the little male whose curiosity and wandering
habits had got him into hot water continually, had made
just one trip too many. The big strong box looked pretty
large and empty with one small lonely kitten beaver
crouched unhappily in a corner of it. They had never been
apart more than a few minutes all their short lives.

I hunted all evening without avail. The train we were
to have taken passed on without us, and it would very
soon be dark. The place was swarming with huskies and
hunting dogs, most of them half starved, and the kitten
would have made no more than a mouthful for any of
them. The chances were poor. Yet I could not believe but
what he had somehow made the grade and got to the lake,
distant though it was. Across a narrow bay I saw a dark
brown object on the shore line, dimly seen in the rapidly
falling dusk – just in time ! I gave several loud calls and instantly, not from the direction of this brown object at all,
but from a spot not a stone's throw ahead of me, came an
answer, a most dolorous wailing. The willows were very
thick and I could see nothing, but I advanced, calling
every few steps and getting an answer each time, until
with eyes bulging and hair erect, the wanderer burst
through the leaves and threw himself at my feet. I picked
up the little furry body and held him close to my shirt,

1. The very young of most animals, as a protection against predatory beasts, are odourless.

while he uttered barely audible whimpering sounds and burrowed his nose into my neck. He was bone dry, so that although he must have been on the point of entering the water, he had allowed himself to be called away from it by the sound of a voice that he knew. Never before, and only once since, have I had the same feeling of relief at the recovery of anything lost.

Anahareo of course was overjoyed. And now there arose sounds of strife as the reunited couple quarrelled lustily over some sweet biscuits we had bought to celebrate the occasion. And as I watched them disporting themselves in happy unconsciousness of any danger past, present or future, I found it strange and a little disquieting that these animals, that had seemed heretofore to have only one use, and that I had destroyed by hundreds, should turn out to be so likeable, should so arouse the protective instinct of a man who was their natural enemy.

From a purely economic viewpoint, I had long been opposed to the wholesale slaughter now going forward, which was indeed almost at an end for want of victims. But this was different. These beasts had feelings and could express them very well; they could talk, they had affection, they knew what it was to be happy, to be lonely — why, they were little people! And they must be all like that. All this tallied with the incredible stories I had heard in younger days, and perhaps accounted for the veneration that our people, when savage, had held them in, calling them Beaver People, Little Indians and Talking Mothers. Indian mothers, bereaved of an infant, had suckled baby beavers at their breasts and thus gained some solace. I had seen them myself cared for tenderly by those whose hands they had fallen into. And I would have left them to die with never a thought, an intention that seemed now to have been something nearly barbarous. Well, we had to live, and anyway they were all right. To make sure I looked inside the box, and carefully securing the lid, went to bed.

That night they gnawed their way out of their new domicile and were found the next morning fast asleep alongside it.

Having again missed our train, with the freakish irresponsibility common to our kind when not seriously employed we decided to miss a few more and stay for the week-end. The news concerning our menagerie had spread, and we were approached by a fur dealer who wanted to see what we had. He made us a good offer. This of course we did not accept; although we were getting short of money we had no notion of parting with them. As I looked in on the two small creatures that were so dependent on me, I knew that never would I sell them into bondage, and that living or dead they should be forever free.

I think it was at that moment that I finally decided to quit the beaver hunt for good.

3

How the Pilgrimage commenced

THIS decision of mine to give up beaver trapping was not a hasty one. Beaver was an animal on which I had depended almost entirely for my living. They had been so identified with my own destiny as to be something in the light of a patron beast, far more so than an owl, a detestable bird whose name had been imposed on me only on account of my nocturnal habits.

One hundred thousand square miles of country in Ontario was dry of beavers, and save for their deserted works it was as if there never had been any. I had travelled nearly two thousand miles by canoe through a reputed beaver country to find only here and there a thinly populated colony, or odd survivors living alone. I had sat in council with the Simon Lake Ojibways and had talked with other bands from Grand Lake Victoria. Waswanipis from the Megiskan, Obijuwans from the head of the St Maurice, wide-ranging half-breeds from far off Peribonka, they all carried the same tale. The beavers were going fast; in large areas they were already gone. Was this then to be the end? Beavers stood for something vital, something essential in this wilderness, were a component part of it; they *were* the wilderness. With them gone it would be empty; without them it would be not a wilderness but a waste. And I, to whom the railroad and the plough were anathema, had done all I could, along with the vandals, cheap fur traders, and low grade bushmen, to help put the country into shape for their reception.

The exuberant recklessness of my earlier days was past and gone, those lonely, wild and heedless days in the vast and empty silences, when I had been sufficient unto myself, leaving death behind me everywhere. I was beginning to ponder more and more deeply on the unfairness and injustice of trapping these animals. The influx of hordes of incompetent amateur trappers that high fur prices had inflicted on the country, I had looked on with uneasiness for some years past as a menace to the profession, and had constantly deplored the brutality of their methods. The regular trapper, if he knows his business at all, sets for beaver only under the ice, so the animal is invariably and cleanly drowned, or else escapes the trap uninjured. A dead animal, decently killed, was no great matter, but a crippled beast was a crime and the woods were full of them.

A number of incidents had contributed to this line of thought. About the first of these was the sight of a mother beaver nursing one of her kittens while fast by one foot in a trap. She was moaning with pain, yet when I liberated her, minus a foot, she waited nearby for the tardy and inquisitive kitten, seeming by her actions to realize that she had nothing to fear from me. Suspended in the air by a spring-pole, I found another female – a beast that cried out in a voice strangely human when I took her down, and died with one of my fingers tightly grasped in her uninjured paw. She had been about to become a mother. This spring-pole is a particularly fiendish contrivance that jerks the unfortunate creature out of the water to hang there. The animal is uninjured and may remain there for days until it dies of thirst and exhaustion. Frequently birds will pick out the eyes before the animal is dead. These and other methods equally brutal are adopted by unskilled hunters who can get their beaver no other way, and these instances were only two out of dozens to be seen on every hand.

These inhumanities aroused in me a strange feeling: it was that these persecuted creatures no longer appeared to me as lawful prey, but as co-dwellers in this wilderness that was being so despoiled, the wilderness that was so relentless yet so noble an antagonist. They too fought against its hardships and made their home in it; we all, man and beast, were comrades-in-arms. To see them so abused awoke in me a kind of loyalty, so that for me to continue my own operations against them along with these alien interlopers who had nothing in common with any of us, now seemed like some form of treason, almost as though I were a renegade who assisted an invader to despoil his unarmed fellow-country men.

Besides the decimation of game, there were other deplorable features of this infestation. Stealing commenced, beginning with pilfering on trap-lines; soon caches were being robbed of equipment, and trappers came in to their grounds to find themselves without snowshoes, stoves, blankets or traps. Camps were cleaned out of supplies and were left in a filthy condition; even canoes were stolen. The old traditions began to crumble. Men began to be wary and mistrustful; some locked their cabins, a thing that bit very deeply into the old free spirit of hospitality of the real woodsmen. In those days we figured that a man who built his camp in a hidden spot or locked his door, was not only an outlander, but he was not to be trusted. Now, and shamefully, it seemed to have become necessary. To rob a cache was the unforgivable thing, and the odd man was shot. It was a sign of the times – the country was getting civilized.

The little beavers are born any time from the middle of May to the first week in June. Beaver hides are still prime at that season in Northern areas. So the spring hunt is still on, and transients swept through the country like a relentless scourge, invading the territories of others, killing off the mother beaver who are easily caught at that time, and passed on to fresh fields leaving the baby beavers to starve by hundreds. Apart from the barbarity of this method, it had done more in a decade to annihilate the beaver than the winter trapping of centuries. Often the woebegone little creatures, already some time without food, would attempt to follow the hunter's canoe as he paddled away with the body of their mother, wailing despairfully but ineffectually. It is to be said in favour of natives that they nearly always adopted these orphans. But their story had always been pitiful, even to the apathetic Indians – a craving for attention, a clutching of little forepaws, confinement, neglect, and after a few weeks almost inevitable death, wailing to the last with unforgettable voices.

Every year in March, when they sometimes came out on the surface, I had lain in wait for beavers and killed them with a club, and their resignation in the face of death was always disturbing; some of them had tried to shelter their heads from the blow with their hands. One, badly wounded with shot, had swum ashore within a few feet of me, and had lain there looking up at me so that I had boggled the execution most horribly. The incident had haunted me for days.

I was getting sick of the constant butchery, and the sight of the ruined works so toilsomely erected, the accusing loneliness of the empty beaver ghost-towns, and the utter desolation of the ravaged colonies was saddening to any thinking man. But this had not, however, prevented me from going on to the next lodge and setting my traps as carefully as ever.

And now had come these small and willing captives, with their almost child-like intimacies and murmurings of affection, their rollicking good fellowship with not only each other but ourselves, their keen awareness, their air of knowing what it was all about. They seemed to be almost like little folk from some other planet, whose language we could not yet quite understand. To kill such creatures seemed monstrous. I would do no more of it. Instead of persecuting them further I would study them, see just what there really was to them. I perhaps could start a colony of my own; these animals could not be permitted to pass completely from the face of this wilderness. But this matter took some figuring. There was nothing simple about it. I had first to discover a family of beavers not already claimed by some other hunter, and then hold them against comers, by no means an easy task. I would tame them; so far an unheard of proceeding, but I had faith in the crazy scheme, and was convinced by what I knew of our little fellows that this was possible. It was like to be a hungry, thankless job, unless I could locate in a good fur country that would provide us a livelihood, in which case it would swarm with trappers and I would have to be my own game warden, with consequent and highly unpleasant antagonisms.

Meanwhile my equipment consisted of two small beavers and a bill at the grocery store.

I broke the news to Anahareo with some misgivings.

'Well!' I informed her, with what assurance I could muster. 'We got a new job. I'm off the beaver hunt for good.'

'I wish you meant it,' she replied sceptically.

'It's true enough though; I'm through,' I insisted. 'I am now the President, Treasurer, and sole member of the Society of the Beaver People. How about a donation?'

'Donations are going to be pretty thin,' she laughed, 'but I am glad. I never hoped you'd do that. What'll you do now?'

I told her my plans, adding, 'It may go hard with us –

we might have to pull in the belt a few notches. Are you game?'

'Of course,' she replied. 'We'll both work at it.'

Good old Anahareo! Not much on the skillet, but right there with bells on when work was required to be done.

Meanwhile other interests had arisen that might eventually have some bearing on this question of a livelihood. For some time there had been staying with us an old Algonquin Indian by the name of David White Stone, who came from Ontario as we ourselves did. Though we had never met before, we were acquainted with him and he with us, by means of that far reaching and mysterious, but highly efficient moccasin telegraph system, peculiar to primitive peoples, whereby a man's character and history are known with uncanny accuracy over whole territories where he has never even appeared. He was representative of that type of Indian that has assimilated much of the white man's knowledge, whilst retaining nearly all the characteristics of his race. He spoke English and French fluently, but with a marked accent. He was a tall, hard, wiry man, but had the moderate movements and retiring disposition of his kind. He was possessed of an unusual sense of humour, a pair of extremely penetrating eyes, and could howl more like a wolf than any man I ever heard.

In his youth the famous Iroquois raids into Northern Ontario were still spoken of, and he was not at all sure that some bands of them did not lie hidden in some inaccessible fastnesses, planning further mischief. He had assisted in the laying out of the Canadian Pacific Railway, and had been present when Edward, Prince of Wales, with his picked canoemen, had started from Mattawa on his historic canoe trip along the old fur route down the Ottawa River to Montreal. He still believed that in some mysterious, far-off, undiscovered region, there was game without end – and gold. For Dave was a prospector, and the year before had found a mine, at present unstaked and unrecorded.

Now mining leaves me cold as a rule and I know little of it; for though I had followed several mining rushes including the spectacular Cobalt stampede of 1906, it had been as a packer and canoeman only, and I had felt, at the time, slightly contemptuous of those misguided people who were grubbing in the rocks and dirt with such eagerness. But an essayer pronounced Dave's samples to be so rich that they interested even me. Evenings we talked over this mine, and squinted knowingly through a glass at the samples, and pored over maps. And the old man's enthusiasm so fired the imagination of Anahareo, who comes of a family of prospectors, that I think the only thing that stopped them from starting out on an expedition at eleven o'clock one night, was the impossibility of obtaining supplies at that hour.

With some difficulty I persuaded them at least to consider waiting till spring, when we might have a stake, and then we'd all go. That was his plan, share and share alike. Then we'd cash in, get us a good outfit, and head north to take our pick of the wild country beyond the reach of civilization; for we all still believed that there was game 'in them thar' hills'. We all soberly discussed the arrangements that would be necessary for the beavers, who would be big by then, quite as though they were two growing children whose welfare had to be considered in any plans we made. David used to play with them by the hour, teaching them their manners and officiating at their games. I had not divulged my ultimate scheme to him, as I was possessed of a superstition that any plan which was broached to a party not directly connected with it would never be carried out.

It had been raining steadily in that part of Quebec for three straight summers, and living in a tent we were always damp and none too comfortable. The Indians were dying like flies from tuberculosis and other ills that this weather was greatly responsible for. Their hunting grounds had been invaded and depleted by 'railroad' trappers and that they had no longer any resistance against the diseases those that were not starving were so undernourished that civilization had brought to them. The Indian doctor from Ottawa had his hands full, and he advised us to get away from these conditions before we fell a victim to them.

A piece of luck in the shape of a hunting party offered the wherewithal to make the move, so we hired out with them, beavers and all. The beavers became at once the mascots of the party and had a whale of a time, getting acquainted with the sportsmen, cutting holes in tents and tarpaulins, stealing bread, getting into the butter and eggs, and being a general nuisance. We let them go at nights, and they got lost pretty regularly, as we moved camp often and these constant changes in the surroundings confused them. But they always arrived home somehow, entering the wrong tent at three o'clock one morning, one of them clambering over a sleeping man and trailing his wet body from nose to tail over the man's face. This caused a passing sensation and some momentary but caustic comment. Towards the end of the trip the party ran low in provisions, and the beavers were much envied, as, their kind of food growing all around them, they were for several days the only members of the expedition who had enough to eat.

About this time we met up with a Micmac Indian who hailed from New Brunswick. His name was, we will say, Joe Isaac. In my wanderings I have met numbers of pretty fair liars, artistic and otherwise, and of these he was by far the most accomplished. He was a natural and to the manner born; one of those men who holds you in a kind of a trance, and whom you must believe as you hear him, even though after you escaped the spell gradually worked off, and you began to see the light. He allowed it to leak out in conversation that he was a professional athlete. And he was good, there was no denying it; he was a very supple man. He had made his living at this profession, but he took first prizes so consistently that at last he had been barred all over the continent. He was at present merely passing the time till this ban should be lifted, as working, he said, took the spring out of his bones. He had scars supposed to have been received in battle, but which turned out to be the result of a surgical operation. His experiences seemed a little crowded for his apparent years, but by careful calculation on that basis we were able to compute his age at about one hundred and eighteen. Altogether a man of parts.

This is a portrait of the gentleman who was to be responsible for our next adventure. Among other regions, he had been in a district known as Temiscouata, and as it happened he really had. Of this spot he talked long and lavishly. He had boats on the Touladi lakes there, owned a hunting lodge, his credit was good at all stores, and he had friends who would welcome with open arms any friends of his. I discounted his possessions, and discreetly divided the sum of his descriptions by about six, and found that even then this Temiscouata or Touladi or whatever the place was called, must be quite a spot. And it was at that.

Anyway it was a new location, we had never been there before, and it was far away, therefore as good a place as any. And of course there was bound to be a hunt there. I don't know where we got the idea that all of Canada was swarming with game; Lord knows we did enough moving around trying to follow it up. It appeared from what Joe told us at one of his séances, that the settlements there were in an impoverished condition owing to the encroachments of wild animals. The deer were so numerous that they destroyed much of the crops. The fishermen on the lakes were at their wits' end owing to a plague of mink and otter that had lately descended on the country. Saw logs arrived at the mill, after passing through this beaver-infested territory, all gouged up by their teeth marks. There was also a species of man-eating cat for which the Government offered a rich bounty.

'Did you say there was beaver there, Joe?' I asked him casually. Joe settled himself in his seat so as to take up the recoil better, and cocked his lip for a broadside.

'Beavers!' said he, his eye kindling – and then he was away. He was most impressive; it was nice to hear him talk. He warmed to his subject. Yes, beavers were very numerous. So numerous in fact that they were overcrowded in some of the smaller streams. It was said that some of them, on this account, had to live out, and grew as a protection short hair on their tails, like otters. These specimens, it appeared, were known as 'grass beaver'.

This Temiscouata being near his native territory, he had not perhaps, for that reason, viewed it through quite the same golden haze that adorned the more distant areas, and some little part of his description was supported by fact. Otherwise this story could not have been written. But the discrepancies were many and varied. His yarns were attractive, I'll say that for them, and well told too. With my conservation idea in mind, I was a little insistent in my cross-examining concerning beavers. So maps were got out again, routes were drawn with sticks in the sand, and we talked and ate Temiscouata and Touladi for about a week.

Trappers' tales! How well we know them, how we love to hear them – and tell them! How, knowing better, do we delight to sail away on some wild goose chase that promises little profit and much adventure – because Peter Handspike says he knew a hunter who was in a country where beavers were so thick, mind you, and the cuttings so heavy and piled so high, that in getting over them a man fell and broke two of his legs – yes sir, broke his two legs and died there. And (here's the secret) no one had hunted there since! And now beavers were as thick as that – (the fingers of both hands held clustered before the face and peered through with difficulty, indicating the closely packed masses of beavers) – and the snowshoeing was the best you ever saw!

Dave used to stand by and listen to these monstrous falsehoods, chuckling quietly to himself, and although he was the wisest of us all he never contradicted them – afraid, he said, to spoil a good thing.

The fact that these yarns could at best be only partly true, and were only half-believed, made little difference. Always there was the lure of the Unknown, the appeal to the wandering spirit, amounting to a passion, that possessed every last one of our kind to the core of his being. The suggestion was about all that was needed, and a sketchy description or two, to start the ball rolling. A map was considered the choicest kind of literature, intriguing possibilities to be read in every outline. While men openly derided the tall tales they listened to with such avidity, they made hasty and secret preparations to act on them, and took a chance.

Gamblers all – let's go! And so to Temiscouata we went.

Poor old Dave nearly cried when we left. We felt like deserters leaving him, but we couldn't rake up the amount of his ticket. So we said good-bye to our friend, promising to send for him as soon as we had made a couple of good lifts on our trap-line.

We took a complete outfit – canoe, snowshoes, guns, cookery, everything. The beavers went in a tin-lined box with a dish for water secured in one corner, and we had a large bundle of poplar for them in the baggage car. When it became necessary to change cars, I carried them in the box on my back, by means of a tump-line. In Quebec city we fed them on the station platform, attracting thereby a large crowd, and there was talk of 'wild animals insufficiently caged'. We hustled them away from there, and took refuge in a kind of a one-man restaurant, where the waitress in charge kindly offered me sanctuary. The beavers, restive from long confinement and excited no doubt by the noise, commenced to gnaw at the lining of their box, and only ceased when it was in motion. Fearing they would damage their teeth, I rigged my tump line and walked up and down with them. We crossed the river on the ferry steamer, and while on board I had to stand with the box of beavers on the tump-line, while they cried out in long continuous wails and scrambled around, and spilled water down my back. We drew a lot of attention, some of it unwelcome, but most of it friendly. We got a lot of fun out of watching the expression on the faces of those close to us as they tried, without seeming to do so, to locate the source of the crying. One gentleman, being at the time well lubricated, asked us why, in the name of God did we not let the child out of the box like Christian people.

Eventually we were all safely stowed away on a train again. The train pulled out, the beavers quit lamenting, and we began to look about us. To my uneasiness I saw that the train was headed more and more south and east, and through a well settled country; a dismal outlook. Here and there stood occasional lone trees, recognizable in their build as originals remaining from the vast forests that must have once possessed this region, and reflecting in their lonesome and forlorn appearance something, I thought, of our own case. Crossing the St Lawrence had seemed an irrevocable step, and I had felt as though we were cutting ourselves off forever from our country and friends. The hypnotic effect of Joe Isaac's oracular utterances had pretty well worn off, and now, as the swiftly revolving wheels clicked off the hurrying miles with deadly finality, we were penetrating deeper and deeper into what was to all intents and purposes a foreign country.

A train ride was no new experience to me. Under the stern protective discipline of an army, I had seen plenty of territory through the windows of a day coach, and in later days, on the occasional trips made to such small centres as Sudbury and Chapleau, I had considered myself a pretty seasoned traveller. The looks of the country through which the train had passed on these occasions had been of little interest. But this was a different matter; it was to be no joy ride. There was the serious consideration of a livelihood, and there was more than myself to think of. The difference was that between seeing a mock battle in the movies, and suddenly finding oneself under fire in a front line trench. My accustomed manner of living had in no way equipped me to earn a livelihood under the conditions that obtained here. We were going south-east and it would get worse. I looked towards the three living creatures for whose well-being I was responsible, and began to feel considerable doubt as to the wisdom of this venture.

Anahareo looked up from an aperture in the beaver box in which her face was buried, and caught my anxious glance. Instantly she asked, 'What are you worrying about now? We are going to make out all right.'

'But the country, look at it. Is that your idea of a hunting ground?' I asked, supplementing, 'And the train swinging souther all the time.'

'It'll change,' she said. 'I bet Temiscouata is just all bush.'

'Maybe, maybe,' I said.

And the farms, and towns, and factories, and macadamized roads continued to go streaking by, and we sat mighty close together on our seat, Anahareo and I, looking pretty pale around the gills, and viewing with increasing disquietude this country that was so different from our own wild friendly Northland. And the two little creatures in the box at our feet, our sole living tie with the woods and waters that were now so far away, seemed very close to us in spirit. They were part and parcel of this adventure now, members of this expedition that was not just two humans and two small animals, but a little company of four, pilgrims together in an alien land.

We changed trains again at Rivière du Loup, and although we swung due south from there, we began to glimpse heartening, though as yet distant views of purple wooded hills and the glimmer of an occasional lake. We even saw an Indian, but had no chance to speak to him.

Our two small companions in tribulation now began to show the effects of the journey, and the sympathetic conductor permitted us to break some train rules on their behalf, allowing us to turn them loose in the nearly empty coach, where they paraded solemnly up and down the aisle. He suggested that we go into the baggage car with them, where the air was fresher. This change and some fresh water (the entire contents of the cooler) brightened them up considerably. Water and fresh air seemed always to have a more reviving effect on them than food. They had not eaten for a long time, nor for that matter had we, in our anxiety. On learning of this the train crew shared their lunches with us and helped feed the beavers, and I think, between the beavers and us, they gave away most of their dinner. Thus the noblesse of Old Quebec.

This friendly treatment and the sight of big Temiscouata Lake, flanked on the opposite shore by a high green mountain that was shaped like an elephant's back and crowned with pine trees, had a very cheering effect on our spirits. And as we neared our destination we saw stretching from the east shore of the lake, and as far away as the eye could reach, the rolling sweep of a sure-enough, honest-to-God forest.

I loaded the outfit on the wagon that was to take us to the lake, and we moved off. The town was small, obviously a bush town. There were farms on this side, but there across the water was our environment, and plenty of it apparently. Things were beginning to shape up a good deal better. But I had still a lot of contriving to do. We had only about a month's provisions with us, and we would have to eat this winter until we brought out some kind of a hunt. Everything depended on my getting a hunter's debt.

After I had paid the teamster I put back into the pocket of my buckskin coat our entire fortune, consisting of exactly one dollar and forty-five cents.

4

How we came to Touladi

THE town of Cabano was a typical French Canadian village, rambling picturesquely along the lake shore in the lee of a high forested ridge.

It was a pleasant sunny place. The very appearance of its tree-shaded board sidewalks, and unpretentious but neat wooden dwellings, somehow suggested a spirit of goodwill and hospitality. The town's most prominent features were a saw-mill, without which it would have had no reason for being, and a tall stone church that stood high on a knoll above the rest of the village.

As we passed through the streets with all our worldly goods piled on the accompanying wagon, we encountered numbers of people, all speaking French. No English was to be heard, and it was apparent that what little of the language I had picked up in France, consisting of about forty words, would have to be brushed up and the forty words put through their paces before very long. We heard the word *sauvages* – Indians – repeated several different times as the speakers looked us over. Evidently we were objects of interest, but although they were frankly curious, there was nothing impolite or unmannerly in the demeanour towards us of even the most inquisitive amongst them. On the contrary it was characteristic that once, when we tried to pass a group that had been conversing on the sidewalk with the wholehearted vivacity common to their nationality, they stepped down into the road to let us by, while the ladies bowed and murmured their excuses and the men tipped their hats to us.

The far or eastern shore of the lake was solid bush without visible habitations. Across there somewhere was Touladi,[1] gateway to our hopes, the river we had come so far to see. We decided to go there immediately and make camp. A heavy sea was rolling, and a party of people who were boarding the ferry boat expressed concern that we should attempt the crossing in our, to them, frail canoe. We figured to put our canoe wherever a boat could go, and a whole lot of places no boat could ever go, so taking half our load and the beavers, we paddled across and landed in a quiet bay just around a point from the ferry landing. This ferry, under the name of *St Jean Baptiste*, plied back and forth over the mile wide crossing, and was the connecting link between Cabano and a single road that wound for fifteen miles through the woods to another and far smaller town. This hamlet consisted of about a hundred families, and was the last outpost of civilization; situated on the Touladi river, it was also accessible by canoe. *St John the Baptist* followed us across, making heavy weather of it, bringing the remainder of our outfit and a few passengers. Meanwhile we turned the beavers loose for the exercise they sorely needed. They at once scrambled down to the lake where, awed perhaps by the presence of so much water after the rather arid interlude of the past week, they contented themselves with running up and down along the edge of it, and making occasional dashes into the lake and out again.

Not long after, we heard voices approaching around the bend, and the same people who had advised us against attempting the lake, came over to us in a state of the greatest concern as to our welfare, they having lost sight of the

1. Pronounced Toolady.

canoe and supposing us wrecked. They were cultured
French people, and one of them spoke English fluently.
And their expressions of genuine relief and their friendly
interest, coming after the forebodings and utter loneliness
of the past few days, gave me a queer unaccustomed feeling in my throat, and neither of us could find any words.
But when they opened up a basket they had brought and
spread out cookies, and sandwiches and candies, saying
that we must be hungry after our long trip, I saw Anahareo's eyes glistening with tears that were very near the
surface.

The beavers, who had so far remained unobserved,
created a diversion at this point by coming up from the
lake with a view to inspecting the gathering, and the
ladies cried 'Oh! oh! look at the pets. Oh! *voyez les babettes!*' and stooped to fondle them with swift little pats,
and then became afraid of them and ran from them, and
the kittens, of course, scampered after them. Then the
beavers in turn became also a little alarmed, and took to
the lake and splashed water over the people with their
tails, which caused more excitement. So that it was quite
a merry party that day on the shores of Old Temiscouata;
but I fear that our visitors found us very dumb and boor-
ish in our bewilderment. They had a journey to make and
presently took their leave, first getting us to write down
our names in Indian and in English, and persuaded us to
draw each a picture of our patron beast or namesake. So
that Anahareo, who is called Pony by those that know
her, made the outline of a little horse, and I portrayed a
solemn and rather cadaverous looking owl. And as a parting gift they left with us a box full of cakes and a bottle of
wine – 'For *souper*, *pour* your sup-per – think of us –' and
their exclamations to one another could be heard long
after they had rounded the point.

And as we watched them go we did not feel so lonely any more, and these kind people perhaps never knew how much they had helped to cheer the hearts of the two exiles that were out on this pilgrimage – or was it a crusade? – of which the end was not yet in sight. We had not, so far, made even a beginning, and our stuff was scattered all over; so we busied ourselves making camp, and built a pen for the 'babettes', as we had heard some shooting and feared to leave them loose too long at a time.

The lake calmed down and that evening we had another visitor, a man in a skiff who brought us some small trout. He spoke not at all, having apparently no English, but smiled and nodded and offered his fish as he stood in his boat. I endeavoured to thank him as best I could in what I took to be pretty fair French, my proficiency in the language existing mostly in just such polite phrases as were suitable to this occasion. I knew the words conveyed my meaning correctly, but he evidently did not understand me. I repeated, slowly and distinctly, but he merely smiled and shook his head.

'That's queer,' I said to Anahareo, perplexedly. 'I'm saying it all right. He doesn't understand his own language.'

'I guess maybe he does,' she replied, 'perhaps if you tried what you know of it he might.'

'Well, what's wrong?' I asked, getting a little indignant. 'I'm talking French, ain't I, and correct too.'

'Of course it was correct,' she agreed, 'but you were talking Indian.' Well, I had known it wasn't English anyway; but our guest spoke up.

'That is quite all right,' he said in perfect English, 'the mistake is mine. I thought you spoke only Indian.'

During the time we camped there we had a number of visitors, people coming over in boats to see us, some of them, we subsequently discovered, important citizens of the place. Apart from a certain amount of natural curiosity, these people seemed to feel that here were strangers within their gate who must be made to feel at home, and they went out of their way to do it. Moreover some of them came bearing gifts. One brought us some potatoes, another a bottle of very creditable moonshine whisky; yet another supplied us with the names of certain people he thought we should be aware of. A fur buyer from a neighbouring town came across with overtures to trade for the beavers, offering supplies sufficient to last till the New Year.

I had not as yet approached any store for a debt, and so far no merchants had contested for the honour of supplying me with a hundred dollars' worth of provisions on long term credit. This was apparently not that kind of a town, and I saw no sign of any regular fur-buying establishment. The store keepers here probably did not realize that there was such a thing in business as a hunting debt, and I knew that this was going to be a hard one to raise. Time was moving along, and the leaves were already turning; I would soon have to get down to it. Meanwhile I had amassed a considerable amount of information regarding the country. This did not quite tally with the glowing accounts we had heard, but its sources were more reliable. We were told the forest that commenced at the crest of the elephant-like mountain, stretched from the mouth of the Touladi river clear into New Brunswick, and almost to the Atlantic Ocean. This was all to the good. But Mr – ah – Jacob, or Solomon, or Beelzebub, had been a little too enthusiastic, and was astray in a few minor details. He had owned no hunting camp, let alone a lodge; his fleet of boats was non-existent, farmers were not complaining of any depredations by fur bearing animals, though deer did actually steal a little hay and as to man-eating cats ...

An Irish timber cruiser who knew the surrounding

country inside out, informed us that if we went in forty or fifty miles we *might* get a few mink and foxes, and the odd otter. There were, he stated, a few families of beaver at widely separated points; they were the only worthwhile hunt. And I was not to hunt them, by self-imposed, unbreakable decree. It was plain that I was going to keep my pledge under no very easy terms. Anyhow I was now sure of my colony, and with the rest of the fur to work on we perhaps could live.

And now a fresh trouble hove into the offing. The beavers went bald, and in a big way. For a long time they had been rubbing and scratching continuously, day and night, pulling out their fur by handfuls, and in a short time they were as innocent of hair as a pair of snakes, save for a narrow mane that extended out of reach down the centre of their backs. This gave them rather the appearance of the shaven-headed Indians we see depicted in the history books, Anahareo's own particular tribe being generally specified. So we gave them the first of all the many names they later had, and called them Little Iroquois. However, the matter was serious enough. They became listless, refused to eat, and began to fight shy of water, all bad signs with these animals. We sought the advice of a doctor. It was his opinion that we should feed them no more porridge as it was no doubt over-heating their blood, in their inactive state, and might eventually kill them. It was bad enough the way it was. Winter was not far off and they had no coats. The doctor gave us a box of salve, and recommended a well known baby's food that would relieve their condition. He charged nothing for either the advice or the ointment, saying, in his precise scholastic English, 'I am an old soldier; I never take money from any of the boys. If you are sick come and see me, it will cost you nothing. I am always your friend.'

Which was lucky. I had just thirty cents, enough perhaps for the baby food. And today I would have to negotiate that debt. A neighbouring store had the kind of tonic food we needed for our invalids, and the merchant wrapped it up.

'*Soixante et quinze,*' he said. Seventy-five cents. I looked at it. It might have as well been seventy-five dollars. And across the lake our two little buddies were waiting in their misery. We had to have it, and with a courage I had not known I possessed, 'Will you charge it?' I asked. I tried hard to radiate an air of confidence.

'*Mais certainement, Monsieur – en suite?*'

I turned to Anahareo who seemed to have the better ear for French.

'What's that he says?' I asked her. He answered the question himself.

'Is there anything else?'

I crossed my fingers, touched wood, changed feet, and could have used some prayers if I'd had any. He was asking for it, so I took the bull by the horns.

'I'm going in to hunt on the Touladi. I want a winter's provisions.' Well, there it was.

'What part?' he asked.

'The Horton branch,' I answered.

'Oh! yes,' said the merchant, 'nice country,' and reaching for his order book, stood with his pencil poised – ready. Just like that.

I went out of there owing a hundred and twenty odd dollars, fixed for the winter. When we got outside, 'Let's open up the champagne,' said Anahareo.

When we returned to camp we found the little beavers as we had left them, sitting pitiful, silent and naked, drooping in their pen. There was none of the grotesque gambolling with which they had formerly welcomed our homecomings, and when the pen was opened they showed no inclination to come out of it. Carefully we applied the salve, spreading it over their little scabby bodies. This treatment induced a fresh attack of irritation, and their rubbing and scratching at this served to massage the ointment well into the hide. We cooked up a decoction of the tonic. Beavers are an impossible animal to feed forcibly, and we were greatly relieved to find that after picking up a few tentative handfuls and smelling it, that they ate a quantity. Before that day was over they perked up considerably and took the medicated food with relish, and in a couple more days had regained much of their former good spirits. I have never known anything alive having the recuperative powers these two animals possessed. From my subsequent experience with kitten beavers, I now realize that with the heroic treatment that we, in our ignorance, meted out to them, they should have been dead long ago. Inside of a month they had their full complement of hair, and from then on they were no longer subject to fits of peevishness. But this was later. Just now, two trips with a heavily loaded canoe would have to be made into the woods with our formidable commissariat, and as we did not yet know precisely where we were headed for, no further time was to be lost. After giving the convalescents three days to get on their feet, I drew the half of our supplies, and one clear Fall morning we broke camp.

And with a touch of frost in the air, a light mist on the water, and with the golden and crimson leaves falling all about us, we eased the nose of our canoe into the current of Touladi, and our gallant little company of four headed for Over the Hills and Far Away, bound for an unknown destination.

5

How we crossed the Slough of Despond

THE river was not one of deep water and frequent heavy rapids such as I had been accustomed to working on, but was shallow and very swift, and the poling, while neither difficult nor dangerous, was pretty steady. Standing for hours at a time in a canoe, the usual position in poling, can become very tiresome. We were a little overloaded, and it took us a full day bucking the current to make the reputed nine miles to a chain of waters known as the Touladi Lakes. This very welcome change provided an opportunity to kneel down and paddle a while. Another half day in slack water brought us to the hamlet where we were to get the precise information that would determine our further route.

Here again a church, seeming very large for so small a population, was the predominating feature of the landscape. On the outskirts we met the real habitant type, some of them with their knowledge of the world confined to the area of their tiny farms and the utterances of their spiritual advisers. Those that might be aptly termed the headmen of this community were kindly, hospitable and progressive; one of them, despite the handicap of having only one arm, was a nimble fellow who took automobiles apart and made them into motor sleighs, had erected a small electric light plant, and built and owned the ferry boat on Temiscouata. But there were not a few who looked askance at the passing Indians from behind half closed doors or windows, or else stood staring in utter and silent curiosity.

On the river bank was a Company store belonging to the mill owners, and they allowed us to cache our stuff in their store-houses. Inquiries elicited the information that we would have to go in another thirty miles to the mouth of Stony Creek. At the head of this stream was a lake that was recommended as a good location, as the immediate district had not been lumbered over. There were said to be a few mink, otter, and foxes in the country and the lake was the abode of a family of beavers, reputed to be the only one in the entire region. It was noticeable that as we penetrated deeper into this country, so the game retreated before us, spread out, and grew less. We learned also that the river forked here, and the branch that we were to ascend was so swift and shallow that a heavily laden canoe was out of the question, and we must have the bulk of our outfit taken by team over a lumber road that followed the river. Coming from a country where roads and teams do not flourish, I rebelled inwardly at thus having to back down, but a look at the river convinced me that it was the only course. It was not a country where people travelled by the methods we were using, and the reasons for this were later to become very apparent. The team was to cost ten dollars, which we did not have. But optimism is contagious, especially if it be extremely cheerful, and this country seemed imbued with it; so we felt that we would raise it somehow, and we did.

On the way back to collect the remainder of our outfit, we came on to a red fox swimming across the river. We captured him, put him in a bag, and later sold him alive for a ten dollar bill. It seemed somehow like a betrayal; he had been free, like us, and the money had no sooner changed hands than I wished I had killed the poor beast outright, and sold the hide instead. The dealer, who had made a special trip for the fox, was the same who previously had wished to make a trade for the beavers, and this time he made a further offer, raising his bid to a hundred dollars, cash. He was not an easy man to refuse, but the beavers were now five months old and had become so much a part of our lives, that I think no sum of money however large would have tempted us.

They now weighed about eight pounds apiece but were not up to normal size, being stunted by lack of exercise, swimming especially. But their teeth had not suffered on this account, and having outgrown their tin-lined box they had become something of a problem while in transit. Once while we were crossing a lake they opened up their receptacle, spilling out into the lake, and we had to lose nearly half a day waiting until they were pleased to give themselves up.

As snow already lay on the ground, and ice was beginning to form in sheltered spots we could not afford any loss of time; so we hit on an entirely new idea. We put them in the tin stove we had, an oblong box-like arrangement without an oven, lashing the lids on tightly and securing the door. We fed them through the stove-pipe hole, out of which the loud, long, and well-known lunch call would issue from time to time. This expedient was the most convenient arrangement we had so far devised, as they roamed the surrounding waters all night while the stove was in use, and in the day time, when it came time to move, they disappeared into it and became simply a part of the regular load. They got to look on this as their routine, going obediently into their tin house and settling down to sleep on their brush beds. And without this device they would most certainly have lost their lives.

Having made arrangements to have our load go round

by sleigh to the mouth of our home-stream-to-be, we proceeded up river in the canoe. There had been several heavy snowfalls and winter had arrived in good earnest. The canoe became quickly coated with ice, and the accumulations that formed on the steel-shod pole thickened it into a club that splashed water at every stroke, so that the gunnell was a solid mass of ice and the bottom of the canoe was like a skating rink. Under these conditions, standing up in the narrow slippery stern, the usual attitude for the sternsman in poling, was a ticklish business. We had aboard only a camping outfit and the beavers in their tin prison. These few things, including the canoe, could have gone on the load, but our dignity would not permit this, and I think that nothing can be so humiliating to a good canoe as to be ignominiously hauled, upside down, alongside a perfectly navigable body of water. But worse was to befall it, and not at all in accordance with the best traditions. Putting extra pressure on the pole in an especially stiff piece of fast water, my moccasins, frozen and slippery as glass, shot from under me on the icy canoe bottom and I fell flat on my face in the river. I managed to twist clear of the canoe to avoid upsetting it, but the light craft, out of control, swung side on, filled, and was forced to the bottom by the pressure. Anahareo, who was kneeling, rolled clear, head first. Instantly we both regained our feet – swift work to be done, a matter of seconds! Somewhere under that rushing icy flood, perhaps already gone, was the stove and in it the beavers were securely locked without a chance for their lives.

We groped desperately, shoulder deep. Anahareo was swept off her feet once, recovering by some miracle of agility. A beaver suddenly immersed drowns as quickly as any other beast, and we had searched for a full minute. And I think we lost our heads a little for a moment, for suddenly we were holding up the dripping stove between us, and Anahareo was crying out, 'They're alive! they're alive!' while I stood stupidly, clutching in my free hand, as though it were a talisman, the handle of our new tea pail, while the pail itself, with the lid on, was bobbing merrily off with our immediate supply of lard, on its way to New Brunswick. The temperature was far below freezing; the water was icy cold and tore at our legs, so that we were like to lose our foothold and be swept away.

The river-bank was some five rods away but Anahareo, by the judicious use of her pole, arrived there safely with the stove and its now frantic occupants. Three times she ran the gauntlet of the frigid racing torrent, getting all our stuff ashore, while I, being of longer gear, did the salvaging and raised the canoe. Fortunately it was a staunch craft, and although some sheathing and several ribs were smashed, the canvas was whole and the canoe still serviceable.

But we had little time for congratulations. It was freezing hard, and ice was forming on everything including our clothes. We were both soaked to the hide and the beavers in their almost hairless condition were in danger of perishing. Some of the blankets were partly dry, having been in the centre of the bundle, so I wrapped up Anahareo and the beavers together in them, and left them to lie there in the snow while I rustled some wood and got an immense fire going, working on the run while the clothes froze on my back. Once the outer clothing is frozen a certain measure of warmth is possible inside them, but I must have resembled a frenziedly active tin-man, and no doubt the whole business, if viewed from a warm safe spot, would have been highly entertaining to an onlooker. It had been a narrow escape for our pets, for if they had been in a light wooden box they would have been swept away im-

75

mediately and been battered to death before they could have gnawed their way out, or I have got the canoe ready and under-way. Anyhow it was all over now, and such is life in the woods that what with the great warm fire, a cooking pot half full of tea and a pan full of deer meat, we were again happy and as well off as ever; while the two deep-sea divers sat warm and comfortable on new bedding in their tin hut, eating some candies that were reserved for special occasions, and making a great noise about it.

We had lost nothing save the tea pail and a small package of lard, and even two panes of glass tied on to a wash-board were recovered intact some distance down stream. Inside of a couple of hours we were again on our way, partly dry and as confident as ever. We spent most of that night drying our equipment, while our two furless companions showed no disposition to enter the water, having probably had enough of it for the time being; but seemingly hard put to find some other outlet for their abounding energies, they dug themselves a long tunnel in the side of the hill before they went to sleep.

Early the next day we arrived at our cache, left there by the team, which had gone back. Across the river from it was Stony Creek at the head of which was Birch Lake, our final stopping place. Here we received something in the nature of a suprise, and also an explanation of the reason why canoes were not as popular in this country as we thought they should be. Those who had recommended this stream as a means of reaching our hunting territory had told us that it was eight miles long, but had omitted to mention that it was three feet wide and possibly six inches deep.

We could no longer use the canoe.

This was a predicament. It was six miles overland to the lake, there was half a foot of snow on the ground, we had at least eight hundred pounds of freight which would now have to be carried the entire distance piecemeal. The joke was on us.

The country in the immediate vicinity had been heavily lumbered, and the slash, we knew, extended to within a short distance of the lake in question. The green country commenced there and our hunt would lie from there on, so we had little choice but to keep going. Packing is one of my regular occupations, but the idea of taking this terrific carry all in one bite, especially in a cut-over country, was a little staggering. And there was more than myself to consider. I had already had sufficient example of the indomitable spirit of Anahareo to know that she would never stand tamely by and see me pack that load six miles alone. And so it proved. I ferried the goods across and had them neatly piled in a sheltered spot by nightfall, cacheing the canoe on high land out of reach of any spring flood. The next day I uncoiled my tump-line and the fun commenced. A hundred or a hundred and fifty pounds, according to bulk, was the biggest load that could be juggled through that jungle of timber, slashed tops and almost impenetratable second growth, thus increasing the number of trips, and there was also the snow to contend with. And when I set down my load at the first stage,[1] I looked back and saw Anahareo behind me with a load of her own, following faithfully in my carefully chosen footsteps. On her arrival I looked pretty straitly at her, but she was so pleased with her achievement, and was so proud to find that she could

1. A stage is a convenient stopping place at which loads are dumped and they are generally about six or eight minutes apart, that being the length of time that a man can walk with a good load without fatigue. He recuperates on the way back for the next burden. This is the Indian system of packing and better time can be made by this method, carrying a maximum load, than by taking smaller loads and going right through.

be of assistance in this notorious jam, that I wisely decided to keep my mouth closed. Moreover she is a full-blood and can, as I have told her, be very obstinate at times. So she had her way, and I compromised by picking her loads, and shortening the stages, and but for her assistance I am certain that some of that load would still be on its way to Birch Lake.

We packed all that day, back and forth, load by load, without speech or rest save at noon for a drink of tea, climbing over piled up tree-trunks slippery with snow, forcing our way through tangled underbrush, plunging into snow-covered pitfalls – but never falling – until nearly dark, returning to camp wet with sweat, tired and hungry, but with that feeling of contentment and well being that comes with a knowledge of useful work successfully accomplished.

We had moved the entire load of eight hundred pounds a half a mile.

The next day we did not do as well. The going became so rough owing to fallen timber that progress without a load would have been no easy matter. In some spots we were obliged to leave the bank altogether, and walk along the stream bed, stepping from one stone to another, or walking in the mixture of ice and water. It at last became necessary to take out a day and cut a trail, time that could be ill spared; but by the end of the third day the stream wandered away off our line of advance, and we had in its place an old tote-road that offered some fair travelling. We had progressed about a mile all told, and were now pretty well organized. We each had our own pile which we handled in our own way. Besides our main dumps, we had always one or two in-between loads scattered at strategic points ahead. These were the lighter stuff that could be carried perhaps twice as far as the heavier burdens, and on these advance trips we were able to spy out the lay of the land. These isolated loads eventually fell behind, so that instead of having to lose time resting after a stage was completed, we could cool off dropping back for them, again forging ahead with them, spotting out our route as we went, and so arrive back at the cache after a long easy walk, all rarin' to go.

Anahareo was getting hardened down to the job in the most remarkable way. She explained this by stating that she was so lightly built that she had little to carry but the load itself. The fourth day we moved camp, carrying the full outfit a mile beyond the last stage, thus being ahead of our work and not behind it, so as to move less frequently.

That same night our load was sharply reduced. Two bags of potatoes out of less than three that we owned, as well as our fifty pound bag of onions, were frozen solid. Well, that was about two hundred pounds that we didn't have to carry any more. We got considerable consolation from figuring how this helped us. Allowing five more days to get in, at the rate of two hundred pounds a day saved, we had made a net gain of a thousand pounds. It was very encouraging; if we had had twice as far to go we could have saved a ton. Too bad though that it hadn't occurred to those stupid spuds to freeze at the river five days ago; we would now have been two thousand pounds ahead. In the woods a man has often to turn reverses to what good account he may, but this was the first time that I had ever figured myself out of trouble by means of arithmetic.

It could be seen that the country had once been well timbered, and this presaged well for what lay ahead of us in the un-cut areas, but we would have been better encouraged by the occasional sight of animal tracks. But there were none save those of deer which were exceedingly numerous, and rolling fat. We would at least live well this winter, and a well fed hunter is likely to be a successful one. An old lumber camp stood beside the tote-road, and it had considerately been erected at the exact spot where a raging snowstorm struck us, so that neither our goods nor ourselves were the worse for it. Here we discovered a twenty-five gallon barrel, empty and in good condition. This was a lucky find, as it would afford first-class sleeping quarters for the beavers, and would not be just dead weight, as on the trail it could conveniently be filled with the cookery and other odds and ends, and so pay for its transportation in the day-time.

Since we had left the stream the beavers had made no attempt to wander away, and slept with us under the blankets. One would lie with each of us, snuggled up close, nearly always with their heads on our shoulders, or with their noses pushed tight to our throats, where they would puff and blow and sometimes snore, and grumble a little when we moved. Over-tired as we often were during this rather trying period, there was some danger that in our heaviness we might roll over on them, or that they would become suffocated under the blankets. In the barrel they were safe and warm, and owing to its concave interior they were unable to get their teeth into it very effectively. Not being able to see over the top of it, and feeling no doubt left out of things they put up a violent protest at this new incarceration, signalling us with loud cries, and doing all within their power to attract attention. Eventually they did succeed in carving out a large square hole about half-way up. Here they would stand looking out and jabbering away, reaching with out-stretched hands and begging for pancakes, of which they were inordinately fond. And as they hung out over the edge of the aperture, with their droll gestures, and that queer language of theirs that it seemed we could almost understand, so human did it sound at times, they looked for all the world like the travellers to be seen leaning out of coach windows at a railroad depot.

They seemed quite satisfied with this arrangement, and soon came to look on the barrel as their home. When they wished to come out and spend the evening, generally about meal time, they shoved their bedding up close to the hole so they could climb out, and they re-entered at will by means of a box we placed for them. They were as mischievous as a couple of monkeys, and although they slept long hours, while awake they allowed no grass to grow under their feet. They were self-willed past all belief, and they were untiringly persevering in the prosecution of some purpose or other, whether it happened to be the investigation of a box of groceries, or the dismantling of our domestic arrangements.

These two irresponsibles were fast becoming a very material part of our existence, and with their clowning, their bickering and their loquacity, they invested the proceedings with an air of gaiety that would have been sadly wanting without them. They gave us far greater pleasure than they ever did trouble, and the discovery on our arrival that the stove was down, or the dishes hidden in out of the way places, or that a fresh bannock carefully cooked against our home-coming, had been taken out of the grub-box and chewed and tramped into an unrecognizable pulp, did not, after all, seem to matter so much; that is, not after the first shock of discovery was over. The time never dragged while they were awake, for there was always something going on, and we never knew from one minute to another when some novel form of entertainment would be provided us.

There was something infinitely touching in their affection for each other, and their complete dependence on us, and there were moments when their gentleness and soft appealing ways were in marked contrast to their usual rather impetuous behaviour. They gave us the same recognition as if we had ourselves been of their own kind, and we were the haven of refuge to which they came in times of stress, which were frequent, as they were always getting minor injuries in their contacts with these unnatural surroundings. They were hostile to anything they deemed to be an intruder and became very angry at the continued visits to the tent of a weasel, one of them eventually making a pass at him, the agile weasel, of course being in two or three other places by the time the blow landed. And I once brought a small deer carcass into the tent to thaw out, and they both fought valiantly with the body all night.

They were the most adaptable creatures imaginable and were probably the only pets that could have been happy, or perhaps even have survived, under the severe conditions in which they were living. Amphibious animals, they were none the less undismayed by the lack of their natural element, and were content to drink water from a cup which we held for them; though the water pail had to be kept out of their reach, as they evidently mistook it for a plunge hole and continually tried to dive through it, with disastrous results. Being unable to collect bedding on account of the snow which was now nearly a foot deep, they took dry wood from beside the stove and converted it into shavings for the purpose.

As each new camping ground was reached they soon became busy with their small arrangements, exhibiting a workman-like ability to take advantage of whatever materials were to hand, building barricades, finding bedding and sometimes, if not too cold, cutting small poplar saplings outside and bringing them in for food. So that often we were all working together and at times got in each other's way, and on more than one occasion one of us had to stand waiting with perhaps an armful of wood, or a pail of water, while some busy little beast manoeuvred for position with a stick in front of the door. They adjusted themselves quite effectively to changing weather conditions. When it was warm they ran around in the tent, and when it was cold they stayed in their compartment and plugged the window.

It was now bitterly cold and bannock froze solid in the tent most nights. The snow was growing deeper every day, yet we were denied the use of snowshoes as packing on them, with the loads we were carrying, will ruin the best shoe made. The packing was becoming increasingly arduous, and the work of breaking and making camp in the snow with bare hands was a recurrent hardship more to be dreaded than the actual moving, as the tent, continually damp with melting snow, froze stiff as a board the minute the stove was out and was as difficult to handle as if it had been made of iron. The constant grind was beginning to tell on us, and Anahareo was becoming exhausted. I at last prevailed on her to quit the pack-trail altogether and content herself taking care of camp. I was able to convince her, as at this time someone was needed to keep fire all night on account of the beavers. Fortunately the country was blessed with plenty of good wood.

It was getting late and the fall hunt should have been well under way. I did set some traps in likely spots so as to have at least a few of them working, but they yielded nothing, nor had we seen a track or any other sign of a fur-bearing animal since we had left the settlement at the forks. This ill-advised trip began to look more and more hopeless as we progressed on it, but I reflected that we had not covered much territory since we had left the river ten days ago, and pinned my hopes on the country ahead. There were days when we made no more than a few hundred yards between the snow and the bad going, and working as I was, alone, progress was desperately slow. And I now began to be uncertain as to the exact location of Birch Lake, as the country did not pan out as described. A scouting trip ahead revealed no lake or any indications of one, and only a dreary, almost impenetrable slash was to be seen on every side. I later found we had been misinformed as to its location, but at this late date I determined to swing over to the creek, now some miles to the eastward, follow it up to the lake and pick out a good route back to camp.

As I proceeded, the country fell away a little to the north and lake formations were soon in evidence, and after fighting my way through one of the densest cedar swamps I had ever encountered, I worked across to a narrow body of water less than half a mile in length. The family of beavers, a small one, was there all right; in fact the lake would have been little better than a marsh, but for the presence of these animals who had dammed it at the outlet. The lumber-works extended no further than the foot of the lake; a most welcome discovery. A haul-way led back from it, a swamp road that lay in muskeg, which being snowed under, was not frozen and was about as treacherous a piece of going for a laden man as could be desired. Anyway it was a trail, and fairly clear of down timber, and my present passage over it would freeze it down a little and provide a certain amount of solid footing, so I carefully walked over it as though loaded so as to have my foot tracks in the right places. Every successive trip would improve this, so it would get better rather than worse. I followed the road as long as its direction served, and then switched off to a fairly clean ridge of hardwood, and was able to spot out as good a route through it as was possible by moonlight, coming out on the crest of a lofty hill that overlooked the valley we were camped in.

Here I stood awhile, leaning on my rifle and gazing out over the staring white silence. My mind was oppressed by a deep foreboding. Our problems assumed momentous proportions. This expedition, entered on so blithely, began now to have all the appearance of a forlorn hope. I owned what was, considering the apparent chance of paying it, a heavy debt. The jealously guarded stack of provisions we had been so glad to get had now become an incubus under which, tired beyond measure, we now moved at the rate of a quarter of a mile a day, if that; and it hung like an Old Man of the Sea about our necks, sleeping and waking, and was like to overpower us before we finally were rid of it.

Further, at the outlet of the lake there should have been mink and otter signs, but there were none; and no fisher, lynx, or marten roamed the hills. There were a few foxes and weasels but there was no price for them. True, I had discovered a family of beavers, a pitiful remnant of perhaps four individuals that instead of protecting, I might even yet have to destroy that we ourselves might live, and so break my covenant at the outset. And with my altered views this would be little short of murder. Was my change of heart after all only the unsubstantial vision of a dreamer, offspring of the folk-yarns of an imaginative and half-savage people, a chimerical, impractical piece of idealism that would wilt and wither under the pitiless searching glare of stark reality?

And far below I could see the tiny glow of the lighted tent that sheltered all I cared for in the world: a weary waiting woman, and two small orphaned creatures. I visualised our return to that friendly town humbled, dishonoured, and destitute; a town no longer friendly. And on its streets I saw Anahareo pointed out as the wife of a man who could not pay his debts. Perhaps we would be forced to deliver our little friends into bondage, where there would be no more fun, no more pancakes – no more love. I went down with a heavy heart.

But all seemed bright and happy within, and we all of us ate, and the people smoked and relaxed in the warmth of the little tin stove that was put to such a number of uses, and served them all so well. And while it roared and crackled and grew cheerfully red I related my day's adventures: the finding of the lake, the discovery of the beaver house that was to mean so much, and told of the so-good trail we had, and how we were now all connected up with our winter home-to-be. And being started I told stories of the days before we met, of happenings and queer characters in the distant forests beyond the Height of Land, and of early Cobalt days; and Anahareo fell to laughing at the adventures of one Bungalow Bill, who had lived in a shack so small that he had to reach outside the door with his frying pan to toss a pancake. And told the story of how he had once gone out to pick blue-berries, and how he had his two pails full and was on his way back to the canoe when he saw a cyclone coming. He made for the canoe, putting down his pails to run the faster, and got there just in time. Sure of his canoe he looked back to see how the berries were making out, and he saw them, sailing right up into the air in two spinning spirals, drawn up there by the suction of the 'twister'. And then the wind dropped, just like that – (a good sharp crack of the hand on the knee) and, would you believe it, the berries finding themselves suddenly with no means of support, fell back down into the pails again, and not one was lost, no sir, not a one! And we laughed uproariously at the unbelievable tale, and the beavers, who responded to our moods with apt consistency, were greatly stirred by all the laughter and the fun, and came piling out from the window of their caboose and staged an hilarious wrestling match among the supper things so that the tea pail was upset and the dishes flew in all directions, all of which caused a real scramble and more merriment.

And all this did much to dispel the fog of apprehension that was settling on me, but about which I said never a word.

6

How we built the House of McGinnis

EVERYTHING must come to an end, and one night at the falling of dark, every last pound and parcel was stacked on the shores of Birch Lake, where it would all have to stay until the ice improved. Having neither a sleigh nor a toboggan, we made a fire and constructed by its light a V-shaped rig that could be dragged, and loading our camp outfit on it, with the barrel, we hauled it in the darkness over some very tricky ice to the camping ground I had previously selected, and which was not far from the live beaver house.

And that night we slowly dozed to unconsciousness with the one all-pervading thought, the surpassing realization, that tomorrow there would be no trail to break, no more relentless pressure of a frozen tump-line on numbed temples, no breaking of camp in the iron bitterness of a snowbound dawn, no more slavery, no more intolerable struggle. There had been real suffering this past two weeks, and much of the time the journey had been little but a hideous nightmare. But it was finished and was now become experience; and much had been learned. Thinking thus, and unable to rest with these persistent and unsettling thoughts, I arose and threw open the door of the stove, and sitting by its light I smoked and pondered, while all my people slept.

There was now a cabin to be built. The site we had decided on for our winter home was in a grove of dark majestic pine trees amongst which stood, decorous and graceful, a few slim white birches. The grandeur of these impressive surroundings rather dwarfed us and our efforts, and made us seem a little like pigmies, and the results of a day's work looked discouragingly infinitesimal in proportion. But the presence of big timber is always inspiring and this remnant of the primeval made us feel free and wild, and somehow exalted, and it helped us to forget that civilization was, so to speak, just around the corner, and that a scant mile or so away was a dreary ruination of stumps and slash.

But there was little time for philosophical reflection. It was the second week in November, and there was well over a foot of snow on the ground. The frost was in the timber, making for hard axe work. The size of trees required for building purposes were found to be far away, and most of them had to be hauled long distances with a tump-line, on skids. It would of course have been easier to erect the camp near the most convenient timber, but the grove of pines and birches appealed to us. Under these disadvantageous working conditions the shack went up very slowly and as it snowed nearly continuously, most mornings we had to shovel out the inside of the cabin before we could go to work. We were quite fussy about everything: the front exposure, the position of the door, and the way the windows faced; these latter were cut so as to give a view of the finest groups of trees.

Operations were being carried on across the lake from the tent, in which we lived meanwhile, and one evening we came back to find the barrel empty, and two winding and irresolute-looking trails leading in separate directions out on to the lake. The beavers had been gone some time. Our first thought was that, sensing the close proximity of their own kind, they had deserted us, as there was a patch of open water that the native beaver had kept open before their lodge. But the tracks led off erratically in another direction, down the lake. Beavers have a homing instinct that takes them unerringly back to a place they have taken a liking to. Though they have a remarkable sense of direction, young beavers appear to have no idea of distance, and I feared that they had set out for our last camping ground, where they had done a considerable amount of work. If they were persisting in this attempt they would most certainly perish in their half-furred state. But it transpired that they had no particular object in view except to wander, and they had left a maze of tracks along one shore that it was impossible to follow to any definite spot, save by the slow process of covering them all.

Armed with a lantern we began the hunt. We worked as fast as possible, as they had been exposed to the cold a long time and would have to be found soon. We called continuously as we searched and were at length rewarded by hearing a feeble cry at a point nearly half-way down the lake. When found the little beast was headed towards home but was lying there in the slush, having apparently given up hope. It was the male, in trouble again, and Anahareo hurried home with him while I continued the search. Very soon, however, I received a signal that we had agreed upon, given with a light, and returned to find that the other had already been back in the barrel on Anahareo's arrival. Before leaving on this hare-brained expedition, these enterprising adventurers had undermined and upset the stove, so it was some considerable time before all hands were restored to their normal good humour. From then on we took the barrel and its occupants over on to the job with us, having to keep a fire alongside it.

Even with both of us working on the building, it was eleven days before it would be pronounced ready for occupation. Conditions were becoming a little disagreeable in the tent owing to the cramped quarters, the steadily increasing cold, and the fact that it snowed almost without ceasing. So one night we were mighty glad to move into the new cabin. It was at present much like an ice-house as the small stove had little effect on the frozen timber, and the apertures between the logs were not closed. The moss for this purpose, which I had had to chop out in solid blocks, would be some time thawing, and I arranged it around three sides of the stove, so as to accelerate matters as much as possible. On waking the next morning we found to our great astonishment that the beavers had removed a quantity of the thawed out moss, and had made a very passable attempt to chink the crevices as high as they could reach, for a considerable distance along one of the walls. It is the nature of a beaver to plug any air leak or draught into his living quarters, and we were to find that this not only included cracks in walls, but extended to the apertures for doors and windows. But this taking over of a task that I had planned for myself that day was at first glance a little startling to say the least, especially to one just awakened.

All that day I chinked and banked and made everything secure without, while Anahareo built racks and a table, and put up shelves and made all snug within. And it was quite a proud looking place when it was all finished, with its smooth red spruce logs with green and yellow moss between them, and its white plume of smoke streaming up like a banner from the stove pipe, to spread in a blue shifting haze far overhead amongst the dark boughs of the pine trees. We both stood outside watching this column of smoke as it poured forth, which all bush people do when the first fire is kindled in a new cabin. The fire had been lighted the night before of course, but we had not been able to see the smoke. We enjoyed the spectacle. It had a very comfortable look, and gave an air of life and movement to the place. And inside, in spite of the moisture that formed on the walls and rafters as the logs thawed out, and dripped into everything, as it would do for a day or two, we held a small celebration, and if the neighbours had been closer we'd have had a dance. The stove pipe was a little narrow and sometimes when the wind was wrong the stove did not draw so well, and when on such days we inadvertently opened the draught too full, we had a smoke-storm. But that was easily dispersed by opening the door and waving it out with a blanket.

The cabin once completed, I hauled over the contents of the cache, procured a supply of wood, killed and brought in a deer, and then commenced to look over the country. It was by now early in December, and the mink hunt, if there was such a thing to be found here, was about over. So I must depend on foxes, fisher and lynx, if any, and these I went in search of. For days I tramped the surrounding hills, swinging wider and wider each day as I sought for signs, until I was no longer able to return nightly to the cabin. There were a few, very few fox tracks, but of other fur never a hair. With a sheet of canvas for shelter, half a blanket, some tea, flour, grease, and my rifle, I ranged far and wide over hill, valley, and ancient beaver meadow, traversing gullies, crossing small watersheds, and following streams to their head. I crawled through tangled swamps, swung across whole lines of ridges, and searched out every available spot where an animal might pass, killing my meat as I went, and sleeping out where night found me; but to no purpose.

Strangely, I was no longer discouraged. Somehow the matter had gone beyond that, and was now become a joke. I became interested in a detached sort of way, to know just what this country would do to a man. The whole thing was preposterous. Anyway things couldn't very well get much worse, so any change there might be, must, I considered, be for the better.

In that I was wrong. It turned soft and the going got desperately bad. Wet, heavy, clammy days settled down over the land, smothering it; days when the snow packed and sagged, clogging the snowshoes so as to reduce walking to little more than a struggle to shift successfully the weight from one unstable foothold to the next before punching through to the bottom. This was followed by cold that covered the dripping trees with an icy coat, and crusted the snow with a brittle glassy shell that would not support the weight of a man. So that no matter how warily I walked I now broke through at each successive step, and with a crash that jarred my whole body, effectually breaking the steady rhythm so essential to the proper manipulation of snow shoes. The crust caught at the shoes with a jerk, throwing them out of control, and sometimes bringing me to my knees. This crust also precluded any chance of ascertaining the movements of possible animals, as they could leave no track on it. It was as though the very elements themselves were in league against me, and had conspired to our undoing. The purging fires of adversity were not to my liking, and I cursed with exceeding bitterness the country that had brought me to such a pass. Thus will man ever rail against the rod that chastens him, though he may be driven thereby, and to his own profit, from a lifelong lethargy of self-satisfaction. But it is hard to submit, give up the ship, pull down your flag. And that is what I now would have to do; strike my colours. I was thinking of my beaver colony.

I knew beyond any hope of repeal that they must go.

I had made an undertaking to kill no more beavers and owing to a set of conditions arising directly from this vow,

I must now break it. They were the only beaver left in the entire region; there were only four in the house. I would need them all. The cards were stacked, and had been from the outset.

Across the lake from the cabin stood the lodge that was to have been the foundation of my colony – the substantiation of a dream, the fulfilment of a big idea. With the two young ones we had and this small family, I would have asked nothing more, and I well knew that once I had killed them the whole structure of my cherished purpose would topple down and never more be raised.

One evening I made my preparations. It seemed like getting ready for an execution. I took over an ice chisel, some bait, and traps. I made four sets. Every trap does not catch a beaver, but in two lifts I would have them all.

Anahareo stood by; she helped me, handed me the bait, passed me the dry sticks that were to guide the victims to the traps. She was, I knew, moved to the depths; but she said nothing, knowing from experience that when my mind was made up on such matters that it was useless to plead. Besides, it was not her way.

The sun was setting, and shone on the pitiful snow-covered home, the sun that these creatures would not be there to see when the spring came. I dismissed these weak unmanly thoughts. It was done. In two days our debt would be secure. We turned to go.

Just then I heard a sound, a shrill treble voice; it issued from the beaver house, the voice almost, of a child. Momentarily it startled me. Anahareo heard it too. 'Just like ours,' she said.

'The very same.' I listened. Another voice joined, raised in protest. Well did we know the details of this small domestic scene.

'He's eating. Someone is trying to steal his lunch.' This

from Anahareo. Placating sounds, then bleats and murmurs of satisfaction, the rattle of busy teeth.

'He's still got his stick.' She elaborated, reading the story out. 'He's eating it. Gee!' She laughed a little. 'Gee! I'll bet you he's glad now.'

Came a hollow plunge, and the water heaved in one of the newly cut holes: first out, that would be the old lady, the mother. I ran to the set and throwing myself down peered in, the ice chisel poised. With a quick stab I thrust the chisel down into the waiting trap, felt the jar as it snapped. I passed swiftly to the other three, sprung them.

There were no words. We avoided looking at one another. We collected our hardware and went home. The sun was still shining on the beaver house.

I had run my flag back up again.

When we entered the camp, the two rapscallions within stood a moment eyeing us, and then surged across the floor to our feet. Anahareo gathered them up in her arms and held them close, and her eyes were shiny. She is not usually demonstrative, but she is a woman and chicken-hearted; women are that way.

7

How McGinty and McGinnis
opened a new door

FROM then on I gave up travelling entirely. Nothing is more monotonous than time spent in objectless wanderings over a country you know to have been thoroughly explored, exploited, cut, dried, and laid out with scientific accuracy on a too correct map, especially if it be denuded of most forms of life. Moreover, there was never sufficient snow for good travelling. To beings of our kind, cessation of travelling, the denial of that unappeasable urge to see what lies beyond the hills, meant stagnation, and worse, long hours of idleness with their dark attendant introspection.

The beavers were our salvation. By now they had grown considerably, weighing in the neighbourhood of fifteen pounds apiece, and their fur had come in full, rich, and lustrous. Although they were growing up, they were as much attached to us as ever, and still cuddled up to us in bed. Our hours did not always coincide with theirs and they were often ready to rise before we were. We would sometimes lie perfectly still feigning sleep and hoping they would subside; but apparently they liked to see everybody getting around mornings, and would pick at our eyebrows and lips and otherwise aggravate us until, in self-defence, we were obliged to get up. We had to sleep on the floor on their account as they clamoured unceasingly to get into the bunk, and made it impossible for us to sleep there. We could, of course, have put them in their place as animals,

1. Wa-Sha-Quon-Asin (*courtesy of Harrods Ltd*)

2. (a) and (b) McGinnis and McGinty at a week old

3. Rawhide (*courtesy of National Parks of Canada*)

a

b

4. Grey Owl and his Beaver Lodge.
(*courtesy of National Parks of Canada*)

5. Two industrious beavers building their house (*courtesy of National Parks of Canada*)

6. Jelly Roll (*courtesy of National Parks of Canada*)

7. The Moose : 'the most noble beast that treads the Northern forests' (*courtesy of National Parks of Canada*)

8. Jelly Roll dancing

9. Grey Owl feeding a kitten-beaver by bottle (*courtesy of National Parks of Canada*)

10. A portage. The fifth man carries the canoe

11. A whiskey jack eating from Grey Owl's hand (*courtesy of National Parks of Canada*)

12. McGinnis and McGinty a few days before Grey Owl and Anahareo last saw them

but their perception of what went on around them was so extraordinarily clear that we felt that we would not be allowed to get away with it.

That they were very responsive to our moods and extremely sensitive could be plainly seen. A bustle of preparation on our part induced them to like activity; as for instance when we were making our bed on the floor, they would run around us pulling at the blankets, and sometimes make off with the pillows. When we laughed a great deal, or held a more animated conversation than usual, they also became very animated. And I found a little self-reproach, and learned to better guard my tongue and temper, when I found that they kept out of sight, when I complained loudly concerning some pet grievance I might entertain.

The stalemate which had fallen upon us would have been well-nigh unbearable, with its prospect of a further three months of inactivity until the March hunt should commence, had it not been for these entertaining creatures. They did the most unforeseen, unheard of things and were at times incorrigibly mischievous. It often took a good deal of forebearance to view with any approach to appreciation, the results of what they seemed to consider a fair day's work. In their spare time they were always demanding something, or moving some small object from place to place, and we were never really rid of them save while they slept, and not always then. But they seemed so happy with everything, and their laughter-provoking antics so livened up the dull and dingy cabin, that we forgave them much of the inconvenience they put us to. Dave, the old Algonquin Indian, who had kept beavers himself in his younger days, had warned us of what we would be up against, and had told us some incredible yarns which we had hardly believed at the time, but I began to think that he had not told us the half of it.

And as these little elf-like creatures hopped and capered at their work, and ran back and forth or staggered around erect appearing and disappearing in the semi-darkness beneath the bunk, the table, or in corners, there appeared to be not two, but a number of them, so that the place had at last something the atmosphere of being inhabited by a whole crowd of small busy sprites. They were continually emitting queer cries and signals to one another in their shrill adolescent treble, and they made attempt to communicate with us in the same way, and were often astonishingly intelligible. Sometimes they squatted upright on the floor and performed their periodical and very meticulous toilet, or sat with their hands held tight to their breasts and their tails before them, looking like nothing so much as small mahogany-coloured idols.

But towards the close of their hours of wakefulness, there would come a time when all this wisdom and alertness, all the skill and artful planning, all the business and contriving would be discarded and forgotten. And the aura of semi-human super-instinct would quite disappear and leave behind it nothing but two little animals who had become suddenly very weary, and who plodded soberly over to each his human friend to be lifted up, and then with long drawn sighs of vast content fall fast asleep.

These versatile guests of ours accepted camp life as a matter of course in spite of conditions that were so unnatural to their kind. They had no tank but lived precisely as any land animal would have done, getting along quite contentedly with only a wash dish nailed to the floor for drinking purposes. They were quite well satisfied with this arrangement, for though the door was open frequently during soft weather, they made no attempt to go down to the lake. Once we took them to the water hole but they refused to enter or drink out of it, but got off the ice as quickly as possible and scrambled up the snow path back to camp.

Their efforts to carry out their numerous plans resulted in the interior arrangements of the cabin being sometimes grotesque, and often exceedingly messy. The most notable of these was an attempt to build themselves a house. They had taken full possession of the space beneath the bunk with a proprietary air that was very droll to see in creatures so small. This spot they undertook to turn into a kind of private chamber, to which end they one night removed the entire contents of the wood box, and constructed with it a barricade all down the outside, between the bunk and the floor, leaving the end open as a means of egress. Inside the enclosure thus formed they next cut a hole in the flooring, and dug out a tunnel under the rear wall, which when large enough served as a bedroom, though its present purpose was to provide material for plastering the skeleton rampart already erected.

We were not aware of the addition of this mud mine to the domestic arrangements, until one day we saw something coming up and over this rampart, to fall with a heavy 'plunk' on the floor – a lump of mud. A stone followed, of fair size; a little later more dobs of mud, large dobs about the full of a quart measure apiece. Inspection revealed the tunnel, and also the fact that the inside of their partition was well and smoothly plastered. The odd consignments that had appeared on the floor were merely a little excess material that had slopped over. When they came out later they collected this and tamped the outside with it. They were really very economical. Moreover they were well organized, as the tunnel being as yet only big enough for one to pass at a time, they sometimes worked in shifts. When they both were on the job together one brought out the material, and the other took it and did the decorating.

All this explained the mysterious thumps and scrapings, and the sound of grunts and loud breathing that had been heard for some nights past issuing from under the bed. This barricade was eventually plastered completely, both inside and out, except at one end where a small aperture was left open, apparently for observation purposes as the window in the barrel had been. When soft weather occurred, the burrow being under the low side of the cabin, all the drippings poured off the roof down on to it and soaked through, transforming the stiff mud into a thin batter. At such times they would come out in the cabin so plastered with this gooey mess as to be almost unrecognizable, and would disport themselves all over the floor, or try to clamber on to our knees while in this condition.

We had read a book dealing with the building of the Union Pacific railroad in early days, and this construction work of theirs, with its wooden framework and earthen fill, reminded us a good deal of the description given, and the resolution and industry of the Irish workers engaged on it was well emulated by our own ambitious pioneers under the bed. So we now gave them Irish names, McGinnis and McGinty, to be as near alike as possible. These names suited them very well indeed, as they were as energetic and at times as peppery as any two gentlemen from Cork could well have been.

The male (now McGinnis) had a little game he used to play. Every day at noon when he arose, he would lie watchfully hiding behind the corner of his entrenchment until one of us passed, when he would charge violently out and engage whoever it was in mock combat. This tournament took place each morning without fail, and was his one big moment of the day; so we made it a point to be sure of passing the appointed spot when we espied him. Then, soon after the assault, which was always made in silence and apparent deadly earnest, out would come Mc-Ginty to speak her morning monologue, declaiming in a loud voice with many different tones in it.

After the morning exercises we fed them tidbits which they retired into their house to eat, sitting as far apart as possible, and scolding under their breath to ward off possible attempts at piracy. The very audible smacking of lips as they ate often made us wish they could be induced to take some soup, to see just what effect would be produced. They were very choosy too and had individual tastes, being satisfied with no odds and ends or leavings, and if several pieces were offered them from the same bannock, they spent some time in their selection. The lunch disposed of, they would emerge for the day's doings in great fettle, coming on deck all cleared for action, forging around the camp very alert and bustling in manner, as if to say 'Well, here we are; what to do?' And almost always, it was not long before everyone was doing, ourselves included.

The fidelity with which their voices and actions registered their emotions was a constant source of interest to us, and they even seemed gifted with some kind of a sense of humour. I have seen one of them torment the other until the victim emitted a squawk of complaint, and then having apparently accomplished his purpose, the aggressor would shake his head back and forth and twist his body as though in convulsions of mirth and then repeat the performance – so that an onlooker once said that he fully expected to hear the creature laugh.

There is no doubt that they possessed, in common with all their kind, capabilities not usually found in animals, though I much doubt that these could be any further developed in so self-willed and independent a nature; but, prepared as we constantly were for the unexpected, I think neither of us will quite forget the first time we saw them engaged in what is to a beaver his national pastime. I had seen dogs, wolves, and foxes tussle and had watched most of the other beasts, from cougars to squirrels, tumble around and paw at one another like the animals they were. But these extraordinary creatures, not satisfied with the amusements that other beasts were contented with, stood up on their hind legs, put their short arms around each other as far as they would reach, and wrestled like men! Back and forth, round and round – but never sideways – forcing, shoving and stamping, grunting with the efforts put forth, using all the footwork they knew how, they would contest mightily for the supremacy. When one was, perhaps after some minutes, finally vanquished, with loud squeals, the bout was immediately terminated and they would make a few hops and turn their attention to their more sober occupations.

These strictly legal pursuits did not however supply the capricious and enterprising McGinty with quite all the excitement she craved. She developed a mild criminality complex, one of those 'kinks' we hear so much about. Although she had free access to the few potatoes we had saved, and had helped herself to them at will quite openly, she suddenly seemed to get the idea that stealing them would be more fun. She took to going behind the bag and extracting them stealthily through a hole, and could be seen creeping along close to the wall with her booty, no doubt thoroughly enjoying the thrill. We allowed her to do this of course, and enjoyed watching her. Now opposition is the breath of life to a beaver; their whole life training is associated with the overcoming of obstacles, and the great incentive not being forthcoming in this instance, the pastime soon palled.

She next commenced purloining tobacco. We were apprised of this during the night by some very mournful wailing which we had come to recognize as meaning real trouble, and we discovered the bold buccaneer laid out in the middle of the floor not far from the stolen goods, which had been partly consumed. The poor little beast was evidently suffering and tried to crawl over to us but was unable to get her hind legs under her, as though paralysed. We picked her up carefully and laid her on the bunk. She was Anahareo's pet and clung to her, clutching at her clothes with paws, so like hands, that had lost their strength. A beaver in serious trouble will sometimes grip you tightly, and look at you and seem to beg. I had not seen this before, and it moved me profoundly to search some past experience for a cure. I prepared an emetic, but she would not, or could not swallow it. She fell asleep or into a coma and her heart action nearly ceased, and I suddenly remembered a case of opium poisoning I had read about somewhere. I told Anahareo to rub her, rub her hard over the whole body, to massage the hands and feet, to keep her awake at all costs. It seemed cruel, but it was a case of kill or cure.

Meanwhile under Anahareo's direction I prepared a hot mustard bath. We put the beaver in it and her head fell forward into the mixture: we held it up. She was unconscious. The liquor did not penetrate the fur right away, but the feet and broad expanse of tail were exposed to it, and it had an almost immediate, though slight, effect. With her hand under the breast Anahareo announced an increasing heart action. The unconscious animal became alive enough to moan and hold up her head, but drooped again soon after being taken out, and soon the heart weakened so that its beat was almost imperceptible. Anahareo rubbed hard and continuously, and kept her awake while I prepared another bath. Placed in it she came to her senses again. We went at the thing systematically, and the camp soon had the appearance of a hospital ward, as we bathed the helpless little creature and tried to rub the life into her with towels. She was slipping away from under our hands, eyes closed, motionless, sinking. There seemed little hope. We worked over her for ten hours. We kept her heart going, but during that time she had three convulsions. Yet she still lived, and the time of dawn, so often fatal, was nearly past. I had seen more than one life go out on its grey receding tide. At daylight she had seemed to pass the crisis. She began to show signs of returning vigour. Her heart beat strongly; she stood up on her four legs. Then she took one last convulsion and straightened out. I dropped my towel; this must be the end.

I turned to put wood in the stove, and found other business in that direction. I didn't want to see. There would be a heartbreak in the death of this small dumb beast. Then I heard a cry behind me, not a wailing, not a lamentation as I had expected, but a declaiming, a discoursing with strange half-human sounds in it, a long loud monologue as of one laying down the law. And then I turned to see Mc-Ginty sitting bolt upright and making some attempt to comb her wet bedraggled coat. Truly, at the eleventh hour. And then I heard another sound from Anahareo.

It was the first time I had ever heard her cry.

Meanwhile McGinnis had been for some time trying to climb into the bunk, so we restored his partner to him and gave him some attention. For once he would have none of us, but flew to McGinty and smelled her carefully as though to be sure of her identity after so long an absence, and plucked at her and made small sounds, short mumbling little whimpers that we had never heard before, and ran beside her nose to nose, while she exclaimed in that strident voice of her, as was her fashion. And from under the bunk the whimpering sounds continued for quite some time; and later when we looked in to see if our patient was quite recovered, the two of them lay with their hands firmly embedded in each other's fur, as they had done so often when they were very, very small.

This dramatic episode put a period on McGinty's debut into the underworld, and for some time after she was quite exemplary. Any real misfortune seemed to have quite a chastening effect on them, and McGinnis, for his part, had been so good since his misadventure on the ice that Anahareo was quite convinced that he could not be long for this world.

They had contradictory, if not complex characters, with strongly marked individual traits. McGinnis, if reprimanded, obeyed immediately and busied himself elsewhere, only to return to the forbidden act at a later date with an air of the most disarming innocence, again to retire when requested. McGinty had to be practically forced into compliance, and would seize the first opportunity to continue whatever depredation she had been engaged in. As soon as she saw that she had again attracted unwelcome attention, she would start to squeal in advance protest against the inevitable interference, meanwhile addressing herself to the matter in the most determined manner, sticking at it until the last possible moment. Yet it was all taken in good part and there were never any hard feelings, and this wilfulness, with resultant scoldings, in no way impaired their affection for us.

On one point however, they were strongly in accord, and that was in a determination to find out, by hook or by crook, what lay concealed beyond their reach up on the table. This table and its inaccessible contents had had an irresistible fascination for them. They seemed to think that they were missing something here. They were especially clamorous at meal times, and although we often gave them all the food they could dispose of, it did not assuage their burning desire to explore this piece of forbidden territory. They tried by every means possible to them to accomplish this object, and they once succeeded in pulling down the oilcloth cover. The resulting crash of tin dishes must have been very edifying, but this, apparently, was not enough. I had an idea they would eventually do something about it, but was not prepared for what actually did happen. We had never left them alone more than a few hours at a time on account of the cold, but one day, it being quite soft, we both took a trip to a lumber camp some miles away, and being invited to stay the night felt safe to do so. The cook, who had heard about the beavers, was very interested and expressed a desire to see them, so we suggested that he come over. As we were leaving he gave us a good sized parcel of treats for the beavers and said that he would be along to see us that day. As this was to be our first visitor here we wanted to give him a welcome, and hurried home to prepare it.

We found the door hard to open. That was because the blankets were piled against it. This however was the least of our troubles. Beavers can, under good direction, do a lot in a short space of time; in this instance the supervision had been adequate and the results sweeping.

The place was a wreck.

The beavers had at last got the table where they wanted it, having brought it down to their level by the simple expedient of cutting off the legs. We hadn't thought of that; there was always something you didn't think of with these hooligans. The long coveted contents of this piece of furniture must have been disappointing, consisting mostly of utensils, but these had been removed and most of them we found in the den later; some of them were never recovered and probably had been deposited in the far end of the tunnel. Our other fixtures were lying scattered over the floor in various stages of demolition. The washstand also was down and the soap had disappeared. A five gallon can containing coal oil had fallen to the floor and had landed, luckily, right side up. The floor itself had escaped serious damage but was covered with chips, and slivers, and the dismembered trunks of our butchered belongings. The scene must have been very animated while in progress.

Since that time I have been subjected to similar and even more devastating visitations, but as an introduction to what might lie in store at a future date this was a little staggering, and certainly we were in no shape to receive a guest.

Meanwhile these whimsical playmates of ours, interrupted in their setting-up exercises by our arrival, were cautiously inspecting us through the loophole in their fortification, and identifying us now came out, two little capering gnomes that hopped over the piles of débris to welcome us home.

It was no use to punish them, as they would not have known what it was all about, being no longer in the act. We had thwarted their natural instincts and must pay for it.

So we fed them the dainties that the cook had sent while they sat amongst the wreckage and ate them — enjoying the finishing touch to what probably had been the most perfect day of their lives.

8

How we made Christmas

APART from their purely physical activities, the mental and emotional capabilities displayed by these creatures, not yet fully developed, aroused in our minds a good deal of speculation as to where instinct ceased and conscious mental effort began. My reaction towards any unusual demonstration of intelligence by an animal had up till now been much the same. But since the coming of these small ambassadors from a hitherto unexplored realm this condescending point of view was no longer possible to either of us, and delving yet further into this remarkable new world offered fascinating possibilities. Other animals too might have qualities, which while not so spectacular perhaps, might be worth investigating.

The opportunities were unusually good. There was a good deal of soft weather that winter, and creatures of all kinds were very active, and with the new angle on wild life which our experience with the beavers had given us, we thought it might be interesting to cultivate these others and see just how they responded.

Anahareo had made friends with a muskrat that frequented the water hole and was something of a nuisance there, keeping it filled with grass and empty clam shells. He was a fat, jolly-looking fellow whom we called Falstaff on account of his paunchy look, and he used to sit at the edge of the ice and demolish the morsels she put down there for him. He eventually got so tame that she could feed him by hand. We had besides, two squirrels who learned to come when called and jump on us, and take bits of bannock from our fingers.

Whiskey jacks to the number of perhaps a dozen, attracted by this distribution of free lunches, attached themselves to the place and were always on the deck, sitting around unobtrusively and motionless on convenient limbs of trees, all fluffed up, and trying to look humble, and dignified, and indifferent all at the same time, as though any such vulgar thought as that of eating was furthest from their minds. But they had a weather eye on the door, and it had only to open when they all assumed a very wideawake appearance, and some of them would start to whistle a little song, hardly more than a whisper, which ceased immediately the door was closed again. There is, of course, no friendship among the wild folk that will stand up in the presence of food, it having on them something the effect that money has on not a few humans, and if a quantity of scraps were thrown to them, each would grab all he could and fly away with it. They too become very intimate, and some members of the flock would swoop down like attacking aeroplanes at any thing we held out for them, and lift it as they passed. Yet others would light on extended fingers, and taking their portion, sit there for a few moments apparently enjoying the novel sensations they experienced, or perhaps warming their feet.

At first these birds were not distinguishable one from another, yet it could soon be noticed that some of them had a kind of personality, an individual manner or a look about them, that set them apart from their fellows, so that they could be recognized quite readily. They are a light built bird with no great strength or speed of flight, but they make up very adequately in address what they lack in force. If sufficiently hungry they could put on a most woebegone appearance which had a highly desirable effect on the observer, but which was exchanged for a very militant alertness on the appearance of anything to eat. One of them carried this wheedling proclivity to the point that when there was any altercation over some tidbit or other, he would grovel in the snow with piteous cries, and exhibit all the symptoms of apoplexy. This always caused a commotion, and under cover of it he worked his way towards the coveted morsel, and suddenly recovering his health would quickly seize it and decamp. Nearly all of what they took was stowed away in nooks and crannies, from where it was most industriously retrieved and hidden by the squirrels; but as these caches were in their turn consistently robbed by the whiskey jacks, things were pretty well evened up, and everybody eventually got enough.

Yet in spite of their shameless solicitation, these feathered yes-men were engaging skalawags. To have killed any or all of them would have been easy enough, but the idea must have been repugnant to any thinking man. Yet I had caught them yearly by dozens in sets intended for larger and more predatory game, where, caught by the legs, they had struggled their harmless lives out in helpless agony. And as these various creatures followed me, and climbed my legs and bravely ran upon my hands and arms, to sit there in all confidence, peering at me so bright-eyed and intelligent, bodies vibrant with life and the joy of just being alive, the enormity of this unthinking cruelty impressed itself upon me more and more.

Anahareo was very proud of having all these creatures around the house, and they somehow gave the place a lively appearance, and made us feel that we had been accepted as friends and fellow citizens by this company of furred and feathered folk. We attended to their wants quite as thought we had been their custodians, which in a way we were, and at last our wild and ever-hungry family increased to the point that we were obliged to have rules and hours for them, while the beavers occupied the times between.

Yet in spite of all these distractions the days were often uneventful and very long. Fortunately, being both great readers, we had gone to the labour of packing in a number of magazines. They more than paid for their transportation by the pastime we got out of them, as we read and re-read them to ourselves and then aloud to each other. Among these was an English periodical which was evidently intended for readers coming under the denomination of 'landed gentry'. We were well landed, if no gentry, and this particular publication became a favourite with us, not only on account of the fine pictures it contained, but probably also because the conditions set forth in it were so utterly at variance with our own. So we ambled around amid its precise and excellent pronouncements much in the manner of a man who circulates among courtiers attired in his shirt sleeves.

Fits of loneliness for the great free country we had left assailed us every so often, becoming at times almost intolerable, and while under their influence we were hard put to find means to combat them. Anahareo would take her snowshoes and wander in the woods or draw cartoons of people we had known, at which she was an adept. For my part, I often scribbled in a writing pad and along the blank edges of the magazine pages or on packing paper, running commentaries on the discrepancies in some of the nature stories we had read, skeleton descriptions of well-remembered scenes and short impressions of outstanding happenings or personalities we had met up with. By this same vicarious means I lived over small portions of my former life and got some solace from it.

Sometimes we extinguished the light, and opening the stove door wide, we would sit upon the floor before the fire, and the glow of the shifting embers threw red moving lances and shafts of crimson light out into the shadowy darksome cabin, and made strange patterns on the walls. and discovered in them secret new recesses that we had not known were there. And these beams came shining out on the tins and pots and other homely ware, so that they gleamed like burnished copper in some old baronial hall, and turned to rich rare tapestry the hanging blanket at the door. And behind the looming earthwork at our backs we could hear the intermittent murmur of the beavers, like subdued and distant voices from the past. So that the place seemed full of mystery, and we talked in whispers, and watched the embers glow and fade and break and fall apart, in the red and fiery cavern beneath the burning coals. And here faces formed, and little images and imaginary objects took their place and disappeared again as though upon a stage. And the shapes of some of them brought back to mind some half-forgotten story or an incident, or thought, and by them there nearly always hung a tale. And presently, as we remembered we recounted them while we sat within the small red circle of the fire-light.

Anahareo related, at these times, some of the innumerable exploits of Ninne-bojo, the conjurer, who was sometimes evil, sometimes good, at times a saint, more often a devil; a plausible rascal with a taste for the occult and having conveniently flexible notions of honesty, and who still survived in the folklore of the Iroquois, who are Anahareo's people.

And in my turn I told my tales of high adventure, and hunger and feasting in the great dim forests beyond the

Height of Land, and sometimes talked of war. And in the cabin beside that little stove was brought to light much that had long lain buried in the past. So intent did we become in our recountings, and so faithfully did we describe every act and every aspect of the actors in them, that they almost seemed to live again in the fiery amphitheatre, and I think they never slipped entirely back to where they came from, but the glamour of the stories seemed to hang about the place.

Some of these chronicles I wrote down, getting a vast satisfaction out of the job, and I took at last to rolling these records up, and put them carefully away. Somehow they began to seem like old and honoured traditions that would otherwise be lost. Pretty soon there was quite a stack of them. I wrote little stories about our muskrats and squirrels and birds, and would read them aloud to Anahareo. She did not seem to be as deeply impressed by them as I thought she should have been, but we had a lot of fun out of it and she would tell them to the beavers afterwards. Of course they would listen awhile, and then shake their heads and roll on their backs as they always did when we made a fuss of them; and that was about all the appreciation I got. But I kept at it. I found that the English language did not have quite all the words I needed, and I was not above manufacturing the odd one. I stole freely out of the magazines, having no idea of the enormity of my offence at the time; but I was having a high old time, and was beginning to be, so I was informed, something of a nuisance around the house.

It occurred to me, experimentally, and with no idea of seriously accomplishing anything, to take the highlights of all these aimless scribblings and try to weld them into something. For I had noticed that many of the narratives we read with such interest had very little meat on the bone, so to speak, when they were dissected. I had plenty of material, so decided to write an article with lots of meat on it. So I commenced the welding process. This took about a week, and resulted in a production about six thousand words in length, very meaty, and in which I covered the greater part of Northern Canada, and touched with no light hand on nearly every incident and animal common to that region. The beavers were in it, and all our other dependents that lived out in the yard and in the lake, so I felt I had done my duty by all of them.

I read it through repeatedly, each time with a more pronounced feeling of satisfaction, and made many alterations, and then rewrote it, working feverishly on it far into the night. I read it again, aloud this time, to Anahareo and would have read it to the beavers if I had thought they would have listened. Anahareo listened dutifully and patiently, and we discovered several points on which I had not made myself quite clear. I easily overcame these ambiguities by adding lengthy and precise explanations. Anahareo worked with me on these troublesome parts and what one did not think of the other did, and the two of us racked our brains by the hour thinking up any fine points we might have missed. This story was going to be true to life if it took all winter.

These additions and interpolations brought this creation up into the neighbourhood of eight thousand words; no mean accomplishment for a maiden effort. Anahareo once suggested meekly that it might be too long, but I rejected the idea with some acerbity; I had read a similar article in which the author had only been able to squeeze about fifteen hundred words out of his subject. I intended to fall into no such error. Thoughts and ideas could come and go, to be used or discarded at will, but the moment one was recorded it became an acquisition. A story, once it was on paper, became a palace of dreams the structure of which was studded with rich gems. Any suggestion that some of these be extracted for the general good, aroused a state of mind bordering on the mildly homicidal. I copied the effusion all out laboriously, parcelled it up with about fifty photographs intended to be used as illustrations, and made a special trip to town with it, a matter of forty miles. I was not particularly anxious to sell it, but wanted a whole lot of people to read this stuff, and if they paid me, why so much the better.

I mailed the parcel to a war-time address in England, giving special instructions to my agent that the serial, translation, moving picture, and book rights were to be retained, in accordance with something I had read on the subject. And some demon of perversity caused me to specify the very exclusive publication, already mentioned, which catered to the aristocracy.

Such a thing as a rejection slip was quite beyond my knowledge, and having estimated, by close figuring, that the cheque would not arrive for at least a month I started home at once, taking a few things for Christmas, which was close at hand. And as I marched along the trail in the driving snowstorm, I pondered deeply on the days to come.

I had got some stuff off my chest where it had been fermenting for a long time, and somehow the writing of that manuscript had partially appeased the feeling of loneliness and home-sickness that had overcome me whenever I saw, smelled or heard anything that brought quick stabbing memories of the trails of yesterday. For now the North was not so far away. It was in my hand, ready at my call to leap to action in the jumble of words and disconnected phrases that flowed from my pencil, as I lived over again the joys and the triumphs, the struggles and the hardships that had made life so worth living, while my soul slipped back to wander once more, at will, in a land of wild romantic beauty and adventure that would soon, by all the signs, be gone beyond recall. Perhaps too, a man might live by writing about it; I had the practical experience but could I use it in this way?

A feeling of kinship for all the wild that had been growing on me for years, at this time seemed to have reached its culmination. My late experiences with the few creatures that were commencing to frequent the cabin, had caused me to have quite a feeling of responsibility towards them. Though they had not a tithe of the appeal that a beaver possessed, they were by no means the abysmal insensate creatures I had been wont to consider them, and they gave a remarkable response in return for a little kindness.

Lately there had been an addition to our clientele. There was a half-grown fawn that used to feed across the lake from us. He was always alone, and probably had lost his mother. I had myself killed several does close in. This little creature, lacking perhaps an education on this account, had little fear of us and would sometimes cross the lake, and coming up the water trail would pass around the cabin on his way. This was always at about the same hour, every second day or so, and we took to standing outside and waiting for him and he would pass most unconcernedly and sometimes stopped and looked us over. He soon became quite tame, and we could move quite freely near him while he nibbled at the poplar tops that had been collected for the beavers. He was a mighty interesting thing to have around, and his confidence, or his ignorance, or whatever it might be, was the best guarantee of safety he could have. After his arrival on the scene, I used to go far back into the woods for our meat, so that the sound of shooting and the sight and smell of slaughter would not drive him away.

Yet a short year ago I would have killed him with a club to save a bullet. And now I no longer wished to kill. I had beaten and abused the North that now I found I loved, and could I but live without this slaughter, this unnecessary brutalizing cruelty, I would be forever glad. A few clean kills for meat, that was the law of the wild, and permissible. Perhaps this new idea, this writing would provide, but I had no notion how much a man would have to put out of this commodity. The thought of the possible unsaleability of my product never entered my head. A man may do a lot of thinking in forty miles, and the familiar setting of the whirling snow seemed somehow to clarify my mind, and as I plodded onwards my aims began to take on shape and form.

My impulsive action in springing the beaver traps I had not regretted in the light of sober reflection. They were now safe. This decision was final and unchangeable. That I could tame these animals I was assured, nor was I wrong. Those other little beasts, the squirrels, the whiskey jacks, the muskrat, the little deer, they seemed to sense a sanctuary and trusted us, and the daily development of their confidence and the manifestations that accompanied it, were an absorbing study. They were more fun alive than dead, and perhaps if I could write about them they would provide many times over the value of their miserable little hides, beaver included, and still be there as good friends as ever. A man didn't need much of a hunting ground that way. I realized that these radical departures from my life training would require something more than the ordinary resourcefulness and physical courage of the woods to bring to a successful conclusion; but I did not know, at least so far as my new-born literary aspirations were concerned, that I was gaily disporting myself where an angel would have worn a life-buoy.

I arrived home in the thick of the blizzard and found the little cabin mighty snug to come into out of the tempest. Anahareo had busied herself crocheting bright wool borders on white sugar bags, split open and freshly laundered, and we now had these for window curtains, which gave everything a real cosy, homey appearance.

The beavers, so Anahareo said, had missed me. McGinnis especially had seemed to search for something, and had spent much time at the door, looking up at it. Neither of them was in evidence, but a nose was visible at the peep-hole in the redoubt and being at length satisfied as to my identity, they came bouncing out and capered round me in a great access of spirits, McGinnis repeatedly throwing himself at my feet until, kneeling down, I offered them the sticks of candy I had for them, and which they sat and ate with loud and most unmannerly sounds of satisfaction.

I laid out my small purchases which the kindly store-keeper had suggested that I make, saying as he did so that it must be lonesome in the woods and that he liked to feel that we had Christmas back there too. And being now in a country where Christmas was recognized as a real festival, we decided that we ought to make all the good cheer we could and so forget our troubles for a while.

I whittled out some boards of dry cedar, painted them with Indian designs and attached them to the sides and tops of the windows where they looked, if not too closely inspected, like plaques of beadwork. We painted hanging ornaments with tribal emblems and hung them in places where the light fell on them. We laid two rugs of deerskin; these were immediately seized as play-toys by the two Macs, and had to be nailed down, when the beavers compromised by pulling handfuls of hair out of them; a pleasing pastime. Having killed a large eagle in my travels, I made a war-bonnet, a brave affair of paint and eagle feathers and imitation bead work, that sat on a wooden block carved in the semblance of a warrior's face, and painted with the Friendship Sign in case we had a guest. It had quite an imposing effect as it stood on the table, at one end. We distributed coloured candles in prominent places, and hung a Japanese lantern from the rafter. Viewed from the outside, through a window, the interior exhibited a very pleasing appearance, though a little like the abode of some goblin whose tastes were torn between the pious and the savage.

On Christmas Eve all was ready. But there was one thing missing; Anahareo decided that the beavers were to have a Christmas Tree. So while I lit the lantern and arranged the candles so their light fell on the decorations to the best advantage, and put apples and oranges and nuts in dishes on the table, and tended the saddle of deer meat that sizzled alongside of the factory-made Christmas pudding that was boiling on top of the little stove, Anahareo took axe and snowshoes and went out into the starry Christmas night.

She was gone a little longer than I expected, and on looking out I saw her standing in rapt attention, listening. I asked her what she heard.

'Listen.' She spoke softly. 'Hear the Christmas Bells,' and pointed upwards.

I listened. A light breeze had sprung up and was flowing, humming in the pine tops far above; whispering at first then swelling louder in low undulating waves of sound, and sinking to a murmur; ascending to a deep strong wavering note, fading again to a whisper. The Carrillons of the Pine Trees; our Christmas Bells.

Anahareo had got a fine balsam fir, a very picture of a Christmas tree, which she wedged upright in a crevice in the floor poles. On top of it she put a lighted candle, and on the limbs tied candles, and pieces of apple and small delicacies from the table, so they hung there by strings and could be reached.

The beavers viewed these preparations with no particular enthusiasm, but before long, attracted by the odour of the tree, they found the hanging tidbits and sampled them, and soon were busy cutting the strings and pulling them down and eating them with great gusto. And we set our own feast on the table, and as we ate we watched them. They soon consumed all there was on the tree, and as these were replaced the now thoroughly aroused little creatures stood up on their hind legs and grabbed and pulled at their presents, and stole choice morsels from one another, pushing and shoving so that one would sometimes fall and scramble to his feet again as hastily as possible, for fear everything would be gone before he got up, while they screeched and chattered and squealed in their excitement. And we forgot our supper, and laughed and called out at them, and they would run to us excitedly and back to the tree with little squawks as if to say 'Looky! what we found!' And when they could eat no more they commenced to carry away provision against the morrow, sometimes between their teeth, on all fours, or staggering along erect with some prized tidbit clutched tightly in their arms, each apparently bent on getting all that could be got while it lasted. And when we thought they had enough and no longer made replacements, McGinty, the wise and the thrifty, pulled down the tree and started away with it, as though she figured on another crop appearing later and had decided to corner the source of supply.

It was the best fun of the evening, and instead of us making a festival for them, they made one for us, and provided us with a Christmas entertainment such as had never before been seen in any other home, I'm pretty sure.

Stuffed to the ears, and having a goodly supply cached beyond the barricade, the revellers, tired now, soon went behind it too. Heavy sighs and mumbles of contentment came up from the hidden chamber beneath the bunk and soon, surrounded by all the Christmas Cheer they had collected, they fell asleep.

And after they were gone a silence fell upon us and all was quiet. And the stove began to be cold : and the place was suddenly so lonely, and the painted brave looked out so soberly at us from under his feathered bonnet, that I put on a rousing, crackling fire, and drew out from its hiding place a bottle of very good red wine that was to have been kept for New Year's.

And we drank a toast to the beavers in their silent house across the lake, and to the friendly muskrats in their little mud hut and all our birds and beasts, and to McGinnis and McGinty, who now lay snoring in the midst of plenty; and another to the solemn wooden Indian, and yet another to the good Frenchman who had supplied the wine.

And as we pledged each other with a last one, we declared that never was there such a Christmas anywhere in all the Province of Quebec. And certainly there never had been on this lake before.

9

How we came to the Depths

IN March there being, in that country, no longer any frost that could penetrate the stout walls of our shack, we decided to go out and collect our cheque. And sure enough there was one, and for a good substantial sum, from the British periodical I had selected as the rather unlikely target for my first shot at the authoring business. Under separate cover was a complimentary copy. In it was the article, reduced to about a quarter of its original length and illustrated by about five of my fifty photographs. I remember being a little hurt about this reduction at the time. When we turned to the page indicated and saw, in actual print in that royal-looking magazine, the words and phrases that had been produced under such difficulties and in such humble surroundings, and saw depicted there our cabin, the beaver dam, and McGinnis and McGinty themselves, we were so astonished that we could only grab the pages from one another and gaze unbelievingly at them, and sometimes bumped our heads as we tried to look at them together. Eventually, with a modesty more becoming to a newly hatched author, I allowed Anahareo to have it for herself, while I examined for the twentieth time the bright-tinted and beautifully engraved cheque. It certainly had a very comforting appearance and would take care of a large part of our indebtedness.

As I considered this pink slip of paper I was conscious of an indescribable feeling of freedom, of having stepped through some dark and long closed door into a new, un-mapped territory that lay waiting with all its unknown and untried possibilities.

But there was more to it than that. The editor had writ-ten me a kind and personal letter, and in it he stated that he was prepared to consider more work of this nature. What I had hardly dared hope for had actually come to pass, and with no fuss, no ceremony. And so, on account of what had seemed to be a foolish, idle pastime contrived in the heavy hours of despondency, the dawn had broken suddenly, bewilderingly bright and clear before us. And be-fore I wrote accepting this new commission, I went out from the small hotel and bought me a fat yellow fountain pen, some ink and much paper, and a new Kodak for Ana-hareo. And when he heard the news the generous store keeper, whom now we almost looked on as a patron saint, slapped me on the shoulder and gave his congratulations in the hearty fashion of a Frenchman, and said that he had known all along that something wonderful would come of it. My own feelings were not a little mixed. This corres-pondence was my first contact with a world that had been as far removed from my grasp as was the throne of Egypt, and while I hid my pride as best I could, and kept my light as dim as possible, you may be sure I did not go around with a bushel basket over my head to hide it.

On the forty mile journey home through the bright snow-bound forest, we walked lightly, Anahareo and I, lifted out of our sombre silent habits of the trail by the good fortune that had befallen us. And we travelled, not in single file as usually, but side by side as we talked and planned for the future, and figured how we would soon be-gin to tame whoever would remain at home of the beaver family that had been so providentially saved.

We decided to build a kind of beaver house on the lake

for our two Irishmen, to give them a start. They, and the neighbourly muskrats, and the squirrels and birds, and the little fawn were to share in our new prosperity; and encouraged by our success with these smaller creatures we said that we must now also find a moose. And we would get together a few belongings, and improve the cabin, and cultivate our horned and furred and feathered friends and I would write about them, while Anahareo would supply the illustrations with her new camera. There were no trappers to encroach and destroy, and the beavers would mingle together and increase and fill the pond and spread, and populate the empty streams round about, and the house of McGinnis, as the lumberjacks for miles around now called our camp, would be the centre, and perhaps become a celebrated place.

We had been five nights away from home, but the frost had been light and moreover we had protected the legs of the bunk, the washstand, and the table (on one stout centre leg now, and therefore harder to cut down, and also easier to repair) with spare stove piping, and had piled everything on these armoured retreats and on the shelves, so we felt no misgivings.

A few miles from camp we found strange snowshoe tracks turning in on our trail. We had no idea who this might be, and always on the watch, we now dropped all discussion and fell into the loping trot we sometimes used. We had had many visitors from surrounding lumber camps on account of the beavers, but not from this particular direction, nor out of the solid bush as in this case, for your lumberjack sticks pretty closely to his roads. This man, as could be ascertained, did not straddle on his webs as does a white man but walked close-footed, like an Indian. This might prove interesting; we hurried. There was a light in the cabin, and not knowing who to expect we opened the door; and there standing before us, with the broadest of smiles and an outstretched hand, was David White Stone, the old Algonquin. He had made the grade.

It was quite a reunion. I don't know when we had been quite so glad to see anyone. He still had the famous gun that could so unerringly pick one man out of a crowd, having been lucky enough to catch a short moose hunt with some sportsmen. He had been trapping all winter on the borders of New Brunswick, thirty odd miles away, and having found a pocket of beavers had done fairly well.

We had supper, and after everything had been talked over and conversation had died down a little, we began to call McGinty and McGinnis who had, for some reason, not showed up yet, although subdued sounds could be heard from them. Whereupon David looked at Anahareo and winked slyly with both eyes like an owl.

'They got business in there I guess,' he said with a knowing grin and another double-barrelled wink. 'I've not been idle since I came; here's a present for you.'

And reaching behind the partition he pulled out one after the other two full grown beavers, still wet and – dead.

Anahareo let slip the spoon she was wiping and it fell with a little clatter on the floor. I pulled out my pipe; the tiny crack of the match was an explosion in the silence that suddenly had fallen on the place. Anahareo picked up her spoon and continued with the dishes. After what seemed a long time I remembered that this man was our friend.

'Thanks, Dave,' I said, my mouth suddenly dry, 'where are the others?'

'There's traps down there yet,' he replied.

I lit the lantern.

'Let's go look at them now,' I said.

When we were outside, Dave, sensing a discordance

somewhere asked, 'What's the matter, Archie? Seems like I've done wrong or something.'

He would never know from me.

'Why, no, Dave,' I answered, looking at him squarely, the lantern raised to see his face the better, and at the same time hide my own. 'No, nothing like that – we've been a little unlucky this winter, that's all.'

Across at the lodge we pulled up five traps. David is an old beaver-man, one of the best. The two kittens were both caught.

'We got them all now,' he offered uncertainly and added, 'That's all there are.' He gave me an oblique, keen glance.

'Yes,' I agreed, 'that's all there are,' and looked down at the two half grown kittens that lay lifeless on the ice before their home that so lately had been filled with intelligent, pulsing life, and now was cold and empty in the starlight. There was nothing to be done. The ancient law of claw and fang had after all prevailed. My palace of dreams had fallen and become a heap of ashes.

Sorrowfully I skinned the beavers next day, giving the hides to Dave. What was left I took back across the lake where they belonged.

The thaw commenced, and when Dave suggested that we all go out together and camp on the Touladi Lakes, we agreed. There was nothing to stay here for now save our few pets, who could live without us as they had done before we ever came. So the old man made a sleigh and a toboggan, and when they were finished, one morning at the crack of dawn we loaded up our equipment, with the beavers in the barrel, and the stove as well, and were ready to go.

And Anahareo went down to the small mud hut at the landing to feed our friendly muskrat for the last time, while the whiskey jacks and squirrels perched and ran upon my hands and arms and took my final offerings; and what was left I scattered on the snow. The little deer we did not see again.

We left the warrior with his bonnet, standing stern and proudly at his post, the Sign of Welcome still upon his face; and left the paint work, and the emblems, and the gaily-bordered curtains in their places on the windows and the walls.

And we bid farewell to the House of McGinnis with its stories and its laughter, its hopes and its ambitions, its beasts and birds and spirits, left it standing there deserted in its grove of brooding pine trees, gazing out with its windows and its widely open door, at the empty lodge across the lonely silent lake.

And Dave saw that we were sad, and as he walked he shook his head and said he knew there was something wrong, but never asked. At the outlet he blazed a cedar tree and made on it the sign of the Duck, his patron bird, and in a notch below he wedged a piece of plug tobacco and said some words we did not understand.

Meanwhile, we looked in on the beavers, and McGinnis took this opportunity to make a flying leap out of the window of his coach and fell into the creek which was open. In the ensuing search and recovery the mists of sadness lifted for a while. With White Stone in the lead as chief, our little band plodded and wound its laborious way four days across the hills into the blue distance, on to Touladi.

We were overloaded and the going was bad, so that we travelled mostly at night while the frost was in the crust. Several times the toboggan, top-heavy with the barrel, upset, spilling its passengers out into the snow, which not liking very well they hastened back in again before the conveyance was righted, generally after a lively altercation as to who should get in first, or else climbed on the body of the load emitting querulous plaints of discomfort. They preferred to be in motion, and when the cavalcade was halted for any reason it was not long before the covering was pulled off the window of the caboose, and two brown heads with tiny black eyes would peer out in a most accusing silence. If a start was not soon made they became fractious, not ceasing their complaints until we got going again. I have exactly that feeling myself on a train ride so was able to sympathize with them, but Dave's point of view was that they were getting the ride for nothing with free meals thrown in, and that they should be more patient with us.

Once the road was reached we had no further trouble, as Company's teams soon picked us up, for in that country few vehicles will pass a wayfarer on foot without the offer of a lift. An official of the Company, not willing to see us camping out in tents, allotted to our use a small snug cabin on the shores of Lake Touladi. This camp, known as the 'Half-way', became our home until we should choose to move.

Here we turned the beavers loose, and they spent their nights exploring the new waters, sleeping in the camp by day. We had many visitors, being now only five miles from Cabano, and were very contented, save for the cloud that hung heavy over the hearts of two of us. But this setback had somehow made me more determined than ever to carry on. The sacrifice at Birch Lake was not to be in vain, and never again would I desert my post and let those dependent on me foot the bill. That it should happen again was unthinkable. With set purpose and design I commenced again to write, and got away another article, though I doubted its acceptance for my new pen seemed somehow filled with a melancholy that flowed out of it into nearly every line.

Meanwhile we kept close watch on the beavers, as the region was full of travellers, river drivers and habitants. They were good company on their frequent visits and seemed very friendly towards us, but Dave, who spoke French fluently, overheard more than one scrap of conversation concerning the beavers that put us doubly on our guard. And the three of us took turns to patrol the neighbourhood, so that they were never beyond earshot at any hour. Our charges were not hard to keep track of, as they were always creating a commotion at some point or another. They built themselves a funny little beaver house a short distance away where the water was open and the soil clear of snow. They cut and slashed small poplars and willows in all directions, and their cries and slashings and other uproar could be heard at almost any time. Just about daybreak they would scratch and call out at the door, and being let in would come into our beds and go to sleep. They awoke about noon, and, without waiting to eat, scampered off to the big doings outside. They had made another partition for themselves of firewood, but they did not go behind it much, preferring our beds to rest in, and as beavers live twenty or thirty years it looked as though we would have to spend the rest of our lives sleeping on the floor.

At this time there came to live with us an old man who had for many years trapped muskrats on these lakes. This hunt was his by right and he depended on it. On account of the danger to the beavers his coming meant only one thing – we must move. So David went out to Cabano intending, with his knowledge of French, to seek a job, while Anahareo and I collected the beavers, loaded them into the barrel, and catching a passing team moved everything to a little lake that lay beside the road, still nearer to the town. Here, under some big elms, we made camp, while McGinnis and McGinty disported themselves around an old beaver house and dam that stood at the foot of the little pond. There was plenty of feed and water and these old works besides, and they would be well fixed here until I could locate another colony in which to introduce them. When our work was finished, we went down to the lake and called them. They came racing over and tumbled their black dumpy bodies all about our feet, labouring under some great excitement, doubtless on account of the old beaver works. They calmed down a little to eat some sticks of candy, still jabbering away in concert, telling us, no doubt, about their discoveries, and the new estate that had fallen to them with all its ready-made castle and appurtenances. They were hardly able to contain themselves, and after a few moments of gambolling with us, during which they pulled strongly at our legs and charged back and forth as if to have us join in the fun, they hurried off to their small properties like a pair of kids to a circus, two absurd but happy little creatures enjoying their new freedom to the utmost, and who from now on would live as they were intended to.

It was almost a year since we had found them, two tiny helpless orphans at the point of death, and this celebration seemed a fitting anniversary. And my heart warmed the more towards them as I reflected that in their new-found self-sufficiency and independence, they still retained that child-like attachment to ourselves that we had feared to lose.

Once during the evening they came bustling up to camp, and coming inside combed themselves and talked loudly and long, and roamed around the tent as of yore, evidently recognizing it, which was not remarkable as it had been their only home for half their lives. They smelled at the stove in which they had so many adventures, and McGinnis burnt his nose on it, while McGinty upset the grub-box, disclosing the bannock of which they ate a goodly portion and altogether seemed very much at home in these familiar surroundings. They had their usual petting party and even slept a while, and it was all so like those eventful days on the Birch Lake trail that seemed now so far away, that we were glad to be back in the old tent again with the little stove going and our two small friends beside us in its glow. Soon they headed for their lake, two gnome-like capering little figures that alternately bounced and waddled side by side down the water trail, and we followed them to the landing as we always did, and somehow wished that they were small again.

We watched the two V's forging ahead towards the ancient beaver lodge until they disappeared into the dusk. And in the star-light, the wake of their passing made pale rippling bands of silver that spread wide behind them, and touched the shore at last, and so were lost. Once, in answer to a call, a long clear note came back to us, followed by another in a different key. And the two voices blended and intermingled like a part-song in the stillness of the little lonesome pond, and echoed back and forth in the surrounding hills and faded to a whisper, and died.

And that long wailing cry from out the darkness was the last sound we ever heard them make.

We never saw them any more.

This knowledge did not come to us at once, but was slowly borne upon us with the slow immutable passage of the days. One evening passed with no ripple to break the glassy surface of the water, no eager response in answer to our calling. A second night passed, a third and yet a fourth, and there came no racket on the water, no cheerful chattering, no familiar small brown bodies trotted up the water trail on happy visits. The rain washed away their tracks; their sticks of candy wasted quite away. At the Half-way their small works had been removed, and the unfinished lodge had been submerged and soon was swept away. There was nothing left of them, nothing at all. It was as if they had never been.

That they should follow the spring flood to the mouth of any stream was inevitable; but their return, in a country of this nature, was just as sure.

We followed the stream up to its source and down to the mouth, caving in through snow banks undermined by its flood, wallowing in slush on broken snowshoes, calling, calling – We scoured the whole neighbouring district. We covered the shores of Touladi foot by foot, and followed every creek. We did this until the possibilities were exhausted, while all around us shots resounded and tracks of men crisscrossed in all directions. Anything could have happened; once we found a deer half skinned, the hunters disturbed by our coming; here and there traps were lying set, regardless of season. I doubt if they ever reached the mouth. Tame as they were they would be easy victims, and one man with a club could have killed them anywhere, they who so much craved affection and needed so little to be happy.

The canoe was forty miles away and we needed it to prosecute our search. We walked in and paddled back eighty miles in three days. On the river bank stood the tent poles of our camps. At one we saw a little pen of sticks, made before the days of the famous coach; a happy camp it had been. We passed the spot where they had so nearly drowned and had been saved, passed it swiftly, never speaking. That night we slept out on the beach of Temiscouata, too tired to walk the five miles to our camp. The next day we resumed our search. For many more days we ranged the countryside. We scarcely ate; our sleep was troubled and our waking hours full of sorrow. Often we made long trips to inspect some hide we heard of; McGinnis had a burnt nose and some grey hairs, McGinty was jet black. We found, mercifully, no such skins. We questioned travellers, followed some, one or two we searched. We went armed; we made enemies. A grim and silent search it had become. Constantly we got false leads, and momentarily buoyed up, followed them to inevitable disappointment.

And all the time we travelled we kept some dainties in the tent and on the landing; but no one ever ate them, ever came for them.

And Anahareo grew gaunt and pale and hollow cheeked; her eyes began to have a strained and hungry look. Once she said, 'I wonder what we have done. Anything else in all the world could have happened to us – anything but this.' And again 'We thought we would always have them' and in her sleep she said, 'They loved us.'

And we hoped on long after we knew that there was nothing left to hope for. We sat at nights in the darkness by our unhappy camp beneath the elm trees, waiting, watching, listening for a well remembered cry of greeting, or the thump of clumsy plodding feet that never came, never would come. And we saw nothing save the still lake and the silent ring of trees, heard nothing but the tiny murmur of the brook. The leaves came, and grass grew undisturbed on the ancient beaver house; the pond dried to a marsh and only the stream remained, running slowly through it.

And at last we knew that they were gone forever. And

they left behind them no sign, no trace, save an empty barrel with a hole in it that sat beside the lake, and dried and warped and fell apart, and became a heap of staves and rusty hoops.

And the aged trees whose great drooping crowns loomed high above our heads, standing omniscient in the wisdom of the ages, seemed to brood and to whisper, and look down upon our useless vigil, in a mighty and compassionate comprehension. And in the grove of stately elms the little tin stove was placed high in a hidden spot with its door open, faced towards the lake. So that the small wandering spirits that might sometimes be lonely would see, and remember, and sometimes enter in, as they had done in life when they were small. And so the stove that knew so many tales might learn another and a last one, a tale of which the end is lost forever, a story we could never, never know.

For we are Indian, and have perhaps some queer ideas; yet who among you having a faith of any kind, will deny us our own strange fancies and tell us we are wrong, or say us no.

BOOK TWO

QUEEN OF THE
BEAVER PEOPLE

I

How Anahareo left Touladi

HAUNTED by the memory of our little buddies that were lost and gone, I felt that the task of reclamation of the species to which I had set myself had become something in the nature of a duty. They had influenced the order of our lives. Without them it is certain I never would have put a pen to paper, and though my ability is, and always must be, very limited, the records I made of their short lives and the attitude towards Wild Life that they inspired, were instrumental in paving the way to the recognition which, unsought and unexpected, was to follow. I determined that they should live again, by hundreds, in their successors.

Dave, with his knowledge of French, had got himself a job, but often visited us.

'I'm sure now they are killed,' he stated. 'We can't get along without beavers now; we must get some more. I'll help you.'

'What about your job?' asked Anahareo, with some concern. He had already lost ten days of his time searching for the lost ones, which fact he had not, until now, seen fit to let us know.

'To hell with the job,' said Dave. 'A man can always get a job. But them little fellas – they never meant to go away – we can't forget them like that.' His eye took in the remains of the barrel. 'Their old caboose,' he said. He shook his head, and looking at Anahareo with one of his rare smiles, added, 'You know, I kinda like to see beavers around here myself, some way.'

An old shrapnel wound, rebelling against the rough treatment of the past month, came to life and put me temporarily out of commission. So Anahareo and Dave walked twenty-five miles through the bush into the Sugar Loaf Hills and took two more kittens. There were four young ones in the house, but the old man would take only one pair. He said that if he had to take them all he would kill the mother and be done with it. She would, in his opinion, be better dead.

Anahareo carried them on her back, in a bag, the whole way and they arrived half starved and noisy, two bits of creatures that would have disappeared from sight in a pint measure, and that weighed perhaps three ounces apiece. They were very delicate and had but a tenuous hold on their tiny lives. By rights they were too young to have been taken.

Dave stayed on, giving us two weeks more of his time, to help us raise them, but one, the little male that Anahareo called Sugar Loaf, after his home mountains, woke up one evening with all the power gone from his legs, and gasped out his puny life before the dawn. The other took sick, refusing to eat the decoction of canned milk and bread that had been their diet, and lay with her head in a corner of her box, a small huddle of misery and pain.

To the population, our attitude towards Nature was incomprehensible, savouring to them strongly of heathenism, which perhaps it was; but the townspeople were not long in finding out about this new development, and aroused by our now well broadcasted history some of them tried to help us. We received much advice, and had the sick beaver been a human being it could not have had much more attention. A woman offered to supply us with cow's milk, and two doctors, all there were in the town, came to our assistance. On their advice we accepted the milk, and thinning it down very weak under the direction of a motherly and very efficient old Irish lady, fed it to the invalid. A man and his wife who had decided to see this thing through between them, administered the doses, every two hours, with a glass syringe, one holding the beaver and the other pumping. The effect, after the third or fourth application, was magical. In two days the kitten was as well as ever, and soon began to evince that assurance and independence of disposition that has since helped to make her one of the best known wild animals in North America. For this inauspicious beginning was the first entry into public life of the now famous Jelly Roll, screen star, public pet Number One, proprietor of Beaver Lodge, and a personage, moreover, with something to say at the seat of Government in Ottawa.

We moved our camp to Big Temiscouata, and erected it at the mouth of the creek on which McGinnis and McGinty had had their last adventure, in case they should ever return. And in the slack water at the foot of it Jelly Roll disported herself, made tiny bank dens and queer erections of sticks, what time she was not engaged in galloping up and down the path to the tents. She grew apace, and as soon as she was big enough she commenced removing magazines, vegetables, wood or anything that took her fancy, and acted generally in a manner which plainly indicated a personality well prepared to cope with whatever vicissitudes life might hold in store. She refused to live in the tent, preferring domiciles of her own manufacture, of which she had four or five scattered around in the pool below.

Aside from fits of affection which attacked her in spontaneous and rather overwhelming outbursts, she was totally different in character from her predecessors. She had little of their clinging dependence, and she came speedily to look on us and our belongings as a natural part of her environment.

Our devotion to our animal friends seemed to have impressed the townspeople much in our favour, and despite differences in creed, colour, and language, we were accorded a friendly recognition as citizens of the town. On holidays picnic parties were made up, and landing at our beach spent hours enjoying themselves in the shade of our birchen grove. Jelly always inspected each member of these gatherings, a habit she has retained to this day, and never registering any great approval of any of them, would amble towards one of her numerous domiciles with such a look of disdain about her rear exposure that her departure was always a source of great merriment, and perhaps some little relief.

We ourselves were at first a little awkward with our guests, but their tactful and considerate behaviour soon aroused in us a desire to look and act our best before them, so that we went to some pains to meet them on the common ground of good fellowship.

It was no doubt this innate courtesy and instinctive regard for the feelings of others that enabled the French settlers of an earlier date to get along with the Indians, so that they were often spared while people of other nationalities were massacred without mercy all around them. It was this same spirit that, on our infrequent visits to town, was to be seen even in small boys, who politely raised their caps to a buckskin-clad *sauvage*, and in little girls that shyly bowed and blushed on meeting a woman of a conquered race. On our progress through the streets, women smiled and bade the time of day, while men stopped and chatted; should we be loaded, as was often the case, people stepped off the sidewalk to give us place. This community spirit permeated the lives of these people, and was observable especially in times of stress. When a fire took place everyone helped subdue the flames, and the family, if rendered homeless, found shelter in any one of a dozen neighbours' homes.

Dave had lost his job owing to his frequent and lengthy absences on our account, and being unable to get another, we were glad to have him with us again, share and share alike in the Indian way.

The proceeds of my second article had arrived and with all bills paid and a well-filled cache beside the tent, we had no immediate worries. We pooled our resources, and while I supplied the groceries David procured the meat and fish of which there were plenty in the adjoining woods and lakes. As an interdependent and self-sustaining community we could have existed here indefinitely, but I think we all began to pine for our North country, and most of our conversations drifted around to reminiscences of it and the making of plans to get back there. I could see no possibility of undertaking my own project in this region, and Dave began to be restless, and was getting anxious about his gold mine. This mine was apparently the only hope there was for any of us to carry out our ambitions – Dave's to retire, Anahareo's to prospect, and mine to create a beaver sanctuary. But there were no resources available that would finance such a trip as Dave contemplated. It was now July, and winter supplies and all expenses for three had to be taken care of before Fall, with time allowed to make a heavily loaded trip, with many portages, over a distance of more than two hundred miles. We were all to be partners, and as the mine was Dave's and I had nothing to offer, it seemed to me to be up to Jelly and me to supply the sinews of war. So I watched closely her activities and wrote stories about her, and penned long articles on wild life from the new angle of my changed attitude towards it.

I read these to a couple of English-speaking acquaintances, who were much amused by them, and one of them who had been something of a public speaker persuaded me that they were good lecturing material. But I could not yet speak French sufficiently well to use them in that way. The only place of any account where English was universally spoken was a resort on the south shore of the St Lawrence, known as Metis Beach, and it was far away. But I resolved to try my luck, so Anahareo being willing to take a chance with me, we turned over everything to Dave, packed up Jelly Roll, some provisions and a camping outfit, and took the train for Metis.

We arrived there with the usual dollar sixty-nine in pocket, and soon found that a lecturing tour that was lacking in a few accessories such as advertising expenses, a manager and so forth, and for which the only stock in trade was a writing pad full of notes, was not likely to be a paying proposition.

In the first place we had difficulty in getting permission to camp, as people of our kind were apparently not common here. A Frenchman allowed us to make camp on his property, and I then made a personal canvass of the possibilities, at great injury to my pride, and was told that we would have to publicize ourselves. At this we shrunk up like two worms that had fallen into a dish of salt. To give a lecture was one thing: to vulgarly advertise was another. Meanwhile we were getting nowhere. Jelly, used to plenty of water, was frantic in her box and cried continuously.

Two weeks passed, and so sensitive had we become at the bare thought of the whole idea, that we cringed in our tent alongside the unfriendly Atlantic Ocean, while Jelly clamoured and grew thin for this salt water that we dare not let her into. We had a letter from Dave in which he hoped we were getting along well. And so we were, getting along well towards the end of our provisions. I considered wiring our storekeeper, for tickets back to Cabano, which he had guaranteed in case of failure. But this seemed like rank cowardice, and besides, too much was at stake. I decided at last to make a move of some kind, so retired into a remnant of bushland and wrote out a lecture of about five thousand words.

Meanwhile word had gone around the resort concerning our aims, and a member of the family who originally settled there, and who owned most of the place, appointed us a camping ground on their property, where there was a small pond. Here Jelly Roll was in clover again. One of the leaders of the summer colony became interested in our project, read the lecture, and approved the sentiments expressed in it. She gave the idea the stamp of her approval, and graciously constituting herself secretary, advertising manager, and treasurer, went to work to launch the enterprise. Her young sons and their friends sold tickets, while she herself, an artist of no small ability, made and issued a number of beautifully illustrated placards. She informed me of the date and place of the lecture, which was to be in a ballroom, and gave me some sound advice on elocution.

I touched up my material, and on the evening set for the encounter, we slipped unobtrusively into the building by a rear entrance. In a back room we sat awaiting our call, paralysed with fright and wondering if Jelly had upset the milk back at camp, or had got run over by one of the numerous automobiles that infested the country. In either event I would, at this moment, have cheerfully traded places with her. We received our summons, and the march to the chamber of execution was one of the bravest acts of my life. Anahareo trailed along with me as moral support, but it was a case of the blind leading the blind, and when I faced all those people, hundreds of them, gathered in a compact mass in the auditorium, I felt a good deal like a snake that has swallowed an icicle, chilled from one end to the other.

But rescue was at hand. The lady who sponsored us now came forward and spoke a few well chosen words of introduction. The audience applauded her. Silence fell. Zero hour had arrived. I fixed my eyes on a kind looking face in the front row, and suddenly found myself speaking. I heard murmurs; people looked at one another and nodded, seemed interested; gaining confidence I warmed to my subject, and pursued my theme to the end. A moment of pause and then came applause loud, steady, long. My head swam momentarily; all this noise – and for us! A British army colonel arose and spoke words of appreciation; he – I could hardly believe my ears – said that it was not a lecture, but a poem; more applause. Then these people crowded around us, shook our hands, congratulated us.

Other lectures followed. I was called on to speak at parties, in other halls, in the hotels. Always Anahareo stood by. I often think she had the hardest part, to sit there, in an agony of shyness, trying to look composed and at ease, and valiantly succeeding. Some parents brought their children to us, commissioning us to instruct them in a few of the simpler devices used by the Indians in the woods. Some of the small grains of knowledge that we dispensed no doubt found lodgment in enquiring young minds, but much of it, I fear, fell on stony soil. Anahareo, with her shrewder woman's instinct, told them tales of the likeable but somewhat villainous Ninne-bojo, as well as other folk-yarns of her people, the Iroquois. But for my part I forgot that children of a certain age are sometimes inclined to be a little blood-thirsty in their choice of stories, and harped perhaps a little too insistently on kindness to the weaker brethren of the forest. That some of these lectures were not producing quite the desired effect on all present, I was very well aware, but I was a little startled when, in answer to my request for questions, a sturdy young fellow of about thirteen summers rose in his place and demanded, 'Did you ever kill anybody?'

'No,' I confessed to the omission a trifle guiltily.

'Didn't you ever scalp anyone?' continued this embryo prosecuting attorney. I admitted that I had not. He gave me a long, level look.

'Well, I think you're a dumb guy,' said he, and sat down with an air of great decision.

Jelly, at one of these talks, provided the illustrations, and her lively expressions of disapproval of the lecturing business contributed as much to the interest of this particular audience as anything that I had to say.

We opened a bank account. Our camp ground was crowded with children, and Jelly became the most popular person at Metis Beach, and was badly spoiled. I have good reason to believe that she never rightly got over it. To these people, each and every one of them, who so accepted us without endorsement of any kind, mountebanks as we must at first have seemed to them, I owe a debt of gratitude that no words written or spoken could convey. I had not known that people could be so kind.

Dave met us with open arms on our return, and would hardly credit our story. But he had to credit the bank roll and the two tickets to Abitibi provided us by our good friend the English colonel. And we could scarcely realize that now we were free, free to fulfil our chosen plans, free to return to our harsh, untamed, beloved North with its romance, its wild freedom and its gold; free at last to leave this sad disfigured country with its tortured ravaged forests and its memories and grief and tribulations.

Time was getting short and there was far to go, so the next day we broke camp and crossed over to the station. We loaded the canoe and all our dunnage on the baggage car, and put Jelly on the day coach in a well-made ventilated box.

As we sat on the waiting train I looked across Temiscouata, looked at the dark Elephant Mountain that stood so still, so silently on guard at the portals of Touladi. Anahareo was looking there too. Each knew what the other was thinking – back of that towering pine-crowned granite cliff, somewhere, living or dead, were the two little creatures that had loved us; and we were abandoning them – for a gold mine. Quitters!

Anahareo choked back a sob. Rising she took her bundles from the rack. 'I'm getting off,' she said in a husky voice. 'They might come back and us not there –'

My thoughts to the letter. I knew she meant it. There was not time to discuss the matter anyway. I picked up my guns, carefully wrapped for the trip.

'You're right,' I concurred, 'we can't quit like this. But one is all that is needed here. I am staying.' This was no self-sacrifice; now that the words were said I was conscious of a feeling of relief. I didn't care for prospecting, I had my writing to do; the fate of McGinnis and McGinty was as yet undecided, and Jelly didn't like train rides and might even die on the trip; all of which was true and therefore unanswerable. So we got off the train, Jelly and I, after saying our farewells, and I got out from among the baggage one tent, some cookery, and my dunnage, and I said good-bye to my old canoe and whispered to it to carry my people staunchly.

I knew how much they wanted to go.

Dave disembarked, his face set very stern and hard, his eyes troubled, for Indian people do not take partings casually.

'Take care of her, old-timer,' I said, and looked him squarely in the face. Sixty-seven years on the trail – I knew she was in good hands, perhaps better than my own.

'Yes, I will,' he said simply, and stood silently holding my hand for the few moments before the warning cry of 'All Aboard', and with a last strong clasp he winked prodigiously with both eyes together, and cried out as he ran for the now rapidly moving step, 'We'll come back with a bag of gold and paint this old town red!' and gave his old time Indian yell, 'Hey – ey – ey –Yah!'

And that was the last I ever saw of Dave.

I loaded my belongings on a wagon, and hugging Jelly tightly under one arm I went back through the blurred and empty streets to the ferry, back to Touladi.

2

How the Queen and I spent the Winter

I FOUND it hard to adjust myself. At one blow I was bereft of all my little community. Anahareo, who had been through so much with me; Dave, with his troubled eyes at parting; my canoe – I felt stripped, empty, kind of weary, famished and lost, with a fierce gnawing at my heart that would not be allayed.

I was now, my period of war service excepted, without a canoe for the first time in twenty-five years, and felt as must a rider who finds himself suddenly afoot in a desert. But I consoled myself with the thought that it was gone to some good purpose, and was in the hands of a man who was, if anything, more meticulous in the care of equipment than I was myself, and whose skill would never bring discredit to a good canoe. And in the same good hands was the welfare of Anahareo, who, full of ambition and hopes for the future, was faring forth to do her share in the seeking of our fortune, neither knowing nor caring what she might be called upon to face – going far into a country that lay no great distance from Labrador and having a similar climate. But cold weather and storms mean but little to our kind of people, and she came of a nation that had made a considerable mark in history, so I had no real fear as to the outcome.

But I was lonesome for the first time in my life. Yet I had, for a solace, a very cheerful and entertaining companion, the little beaver who, if she was ever lonely, never showed it. No longer a kitten, she had developed into a beautiful specimen of her kind, was always bright and very much alive, and had a rich, full-furred coat, dark and glistening, which it had been Anahareo's pride to groom carefully each day.

To get ready for the winter, I, on advice, located a small camp, well built and in good shape, on the shores of a little lake about five miles back of the Elephant mountain. A bush road led to it, mostly swamp, and hiring a team to bring in our supplies we, Jelly 'n' me, moved to it for a permanent abode, she being carried in a packsack with her head and arms free, viewing the scenery round about on the way in.

What had passed now seemed to be an epoch, a line of demarcation in our lives, dividing the new from the old. And symbolical of the new was this tiny squalling brat upon my back. Little did I think as she sat in the packsack and chittered and mumbled and upbraided and pulled my hair, that she was to become a very noted lady, and was to make a name for both herself and me. Her whole short life of five months had been turned topsy-turvy, inside out, hell, west and sideways. She had been transported hither and thither on trains and wagons, carried long distances in a variety of boxes, had been Exhibit 'A' on a lecture tour, and had finally spent two entire days in a stable. In the latter place, for a swimming pool she had a dish pan, and instead of poplar had been fed pancakes.

And now came the end of this last short, but very eventful journey, to where all was peace and quietness and contentment, to this little lake set high in the mountains where there was plenty of deep water for birling like a spinning log and diving to her heart's content. Here was any amount of mud in which to play and build any number of little imitation beaver houses on the shore, and there was even a long burrow with a roomy sleeping apartment at the end of it, left by some long departed family of her kind. All this spelled a happiness she had never before known, and she had a delirious time for the first few days. She slept in the burrow, which was up the creek about half a mile from the cabin, but every evening about sunset she was at the cabin door, scratching to be let in. She came in several times a night and spent an hour with me, and took a great interest in my doings. She was particularly attracted by the bunk, recognizing perhaps the scent of the blankets on which she had been in the habit of drying herself off. I made a kind of chute for her, and she would climb into the bed by means of this, getting out by the very simple process of falling over the side, and as I left the door ajar on her account, I often awoke in the morning to find her fast asleep beside me.

Meanwhile I found plenty of outlet for my desire to write. During a visit to town I picked up a sporting magazine and I was strongly attracted by the conservation ideas expressed all through it, and read in it an article by a man I had known well in Ontario. He was pretty much of a theorist who wrote greatly from second hand experience, and while part of his information was correct, a good deal of it was misleading. Sitting down in the house of a friend I wrote an article on the subject, taking those of his statements which in my opinion were incorrect as a theme, and discussing them from a point of view of personal observation. It was called 'The Vanishing Life of the Wild', and the periodical was *Canadian Forest and Outdoors*, the official organ of the Canadian Forestry Association of which I was later to become a life member. This was my first appearance in print in this country. They asked me for more, and I wrote intermittently for them for three years.

Country Life, in England, who had had two articles

from me and a series of long rambling personal letters written to the editor during fits of loneliness, now sent me a request to write a book. Nothing loath I accepted, not having the remotest idea of how I was going to set about it. One difficulty appeared to be insurmountable, and that was how, with my entire lack of technical knowledge, to give an account of happenings in which I acted in the role not only of an observer but of an active participant, and yet to avoid an offensive use of the first personal pronoun. So I decided to write, not a personal biography, as requested, but a series of essays on the North itself. In this present work, however, it seemed that a few good healthy unequivocating 'I's' standing up honestly on their own hind legs, would do no harm whatever. It feels a lot better, this time, to be more of a humanist.

At this time a letter arrived from Anahareo reporting progress. All had gone well, save that they were lonesome, seemingly a chronic condition with all of us, and they had been, at the time of writing, ready to leave with a canoe load of supplies for Chibougamou Lake, two hundred odd miles North from the steel.

There had, she related, been adventures in Quebec City. David, bewildered by the number of taverns that were to be found everywhere, had gotten lost. Anahareo, after two days of waiting, started to trail him down, inquiring at all beer parlours. Yes, he was well known at several taverns, and had been feeling, oh, just so-so, when last seen. His ecclesiastical leanings when in this condition prompted her to consider searching all the churches, beginning with the largest and working down. She compromised by making the rounds of the police stations, but none of them had any record of him. She found him in the railroad depot, tired and very hungry. I have it on the word of witnesses that they almost embraced. Dave, it appeared, having lost all track of time, and supposing he had missed his train and that Anahareo had gone on without him, had boarded the first one he saw, and without ticket, money, equipment or anything else except the clothes he stood up in, and a headache, had proceeded sixty miles or so in the wrong direction. Apprised of this fact by the conductor he got off and had walked back. I kind of sweated as I read all this, but by now they were safely away on the lakes. They wanted for nothing, and I knew that once in the bush few men were David's peer.

Meanwhile I myself was busy. Hunting season was open and hunters swarmed in the woods. This made it necessary for me to patrol the scene of Jelly's activities all night, and I slept beside her burrow in the day-time. I much doubted if there were many of the Cabano men who would have deliberately killed her, but as with McGinnis and Mc-Ginty, it would only take one man to turn the trick and I was resolved to take no chances. I was greatly assisted in this by the trapper who claimed the hunting ground I was occupying. Instead of trying to oust me from his holdings, on finding that I was without a canoe he lent me one, and drew me a map of the district so I could patrol the more effectively.

Hunting season passed and the woods became again deserted and we, this beaver and I, carried on our preparations for the winter each at his own end of the lake. The outlet, near which my cabin was situated, passed through a muskeg, and the immediate neighbourhood was covered with spindling birch which I was rapidly using up for wood. Jelly had by far the best part of it so far as scenery was concerned, being picturesquely established at the mouth of a small stream that wandered down from the uplands through a well timbered gully. Here she lived in state. She fortified her burrow on the top with mud, sticks and moss, and inside it had a fine clean bed of shavings (taken from stolen boards), and had a little feed raft she had collected with highly unskilled labour, and that had a very amateurish look about it. But she was socially inclined, and often came down and spent long hours in the camp.

When it snowed she failed to show up and I would visit her, and hearing my approach while still at some distance, she would come running to meet me with squeals and wiggles of welcome. We had great company together visiting back and forth this way, and I often sat and smoked and watched her working, and helped in any difficulties that arose. After the ice took her visits ceased altogether, and becoming lonesome for her I sometimes carried her to the cabin on my back in a box. She did not seem to mind these trips, and carried on a conversation with me and made long speeches on the way; I used to tell her she was talking behind my back. She made her own way home under the ice in some mysterious manner and always arrived safely, though I made a practice of following her progress along the shore with a flashlight, to make sure she did. This distance was over half a mile and I much admired the skill with which she negotiated it, though she cheated a little and ran her nose into muskrat burrows here and there to replenish her air supply.

One night, however, after going home, she returned again unknown to me, and in the morning I found the door wide open and her lying fast asleep across the pillow. Nor did she ever go outside again, evidently having decided to spend the winter with me; which she did. So I bought a small galvanized tank for her and sunk it in the floor, and dug out under one of the walls what I considered to be a pretty good imitation of a beaver house interior.

Almost immediately on her entry, a certain independence of spirit began to manifest itself. The tank, after a lengthy inspection, was accepted by her as being all right, what there was of it; but the alleged beaver house, on being weighed in the balance, was found to be wanting, and was resolutely and efficiently blocked up with some bagging and an old deer skin. She then dug out at great labour, a long tunnel under one corner of the shack, bringing up the dirt in heaps which she pushed ahead of her and painstakingly spread over the floor. This I removed, upon which it was promptly renewed. On my further attempt to clean up, she worked feverishly until a section of the floor within a radius of about six feet was again covered. I removed this several different times with the same results, and at last was obliged to desist for fear that in her continued excavations she would undermine the camp.

Eventually she constructed a smooth solid side walk of pounded earth clear from her tunnel to the water supply, and she had a well beaten playground tramped down all round her door. Having thus gained her point, she let the matter drop, and we were apparently all set for the winter. But these proceedings were merely preliminaries. She now embarked on a campaign of constructive activities that made necessary the alteration of almost the entire interior arrangements of the camp. Nights of earnest endeavours to empty the woodbox (to supply materials for scaffolds which would afford ready access to the table or windows) alternated with orgies of destruction, during which anything not made of steel or iron was subjected to a trial by ordeal out of which it always came off second best. The bottom of the door which, owing to the slight draught entering there, was a point that attracted much attention, was always kept well banked up with any materials that could be collected. and in more than one instance the blankets were taken from the bunk and utilized for this purpose. Reprimands induced only a temporary cessation of these depredations, and slaps and switchings produced little squeals accompanied by the violent twisting and shaking of the head, and other curious contortions by which these animals evince the spirit of fun by which they seem to be consumed during the first year of their life.

On the few occasions I found it necessary to punish her, she would stand up on her hind feet, look me square in the face, and argue the point with me in her querulous treble of annoyance and outrage, slapping back at me right manfully on more than one occasion; yet she never on any account attempted to make use of her terrible teeth. Being in disgrace, she would climb on her box alongside me at the table, and rest her head on my knee, eyeing me and talking meanwhile in her uncanny language, as though to say, 'What are a few table legs and axe handles between men?' And she always got forgiven; for after all she was a High Beaver, Highest of All The Beavers, and could get away with things no common beaver could, things that no common beaver would ever even think of.

When I sat on the deer skin rug before the stove, which was often, she would come and lie with her head in my lap, and looking up at me, make a series of prolonged wavering sounds in different keys, that could have been construed as some bizarre attempt at singing. This pastime soon became a regular feature of her day, and the not unmelodious notes she emitted on these occasions were among the strangest sounds I have ever heard an animal make.

In spite of our difference in point of view on some subjects, we grew very close during that winter for we were both, of our kind, alone. More and more as time went on she timed her movements, such as rising and retiring and her meal-times, by mine. The camp, the fixtures, the bed, the tank, her little den and myself, these were her whole world. She took me as much for granted as if I had also been a beaver, and it is possible that she thought that I belonged to her, with the rest of the stuff, or figured that she would grow up to be like me and perhaps eat at the table when she got big, or else that I would later have a tail and become like her.

Did I leave the camp on a two day trip for supplies, my entry was the signal for a swift exit from her chamber, and a violent assault on my legs, calculated to upset me. And on my squatting down to ask her how the thing had been going in my absence, she would sit up and wag her head slowly back and forth and roll on her back and gambol clumsily around me. As soon as I unlashed the toboggan, every article and package was minutely examined until the one containing the never-failing apples was discovered. This was immediately torn open, and gathering all the apples she could in her teeth and arms, she would stagger away erect to the edge of her tank, where she would eat one and put the rest in the water. She entered the water but rarely, and after emerging from a bath she had one certain spot where she sat and squeezed all the moisture out of her fur with her forepaws, very hands in function. She did not like to sit in the pool which collected under her at such times, so she took possession of a large square of birch bark for a bath-mat, intended to shed the water, which it sometimes did.

It was not long before she discovered that the bed was a very good place for these exercises, as the blankets soaked up the moisture. After considerable inducement, she later compromised by shredding up the birch bark and spreading on it a layer of moss taken from the chinking in the walls. Her bed, which consisted of long, very fine shavings cut from the flooring and portions of bagging which she unravelled, was pushed out at intervals and spread on the floor to air, being later returned to the sleeping quarters. Both these procedures were remarkable examples of adaptability on the part of an animal, especially the latter, as in the natural state the bedding is taken out and discarded entirely, fresh material being sought. The dish out of which she ate, on being emptied she would shove into a corner, and was not satisfied until it was standing up against the wall. This trick seems to be instinctive with all beavers, and can be attributed to their desire to preserve the interior of their habitation clear of any form of débris in the shape of peeled sticks, which are likewise set aside in the angle of the wall until the owner is ready to remove them.

Any branches brought in for feed, if thrown down in an unaccustomed place, were drawn over and neatly piled near the water supply, nor would she suffer any sticks or loose materials to be scattered on the floor; these she always removed and relegated to a junk pile she kept under one of the windows. This I found applied to socks, moccasins, the washboard and the broom, etc., as well as to sticks. This broom was to her a kind of staff of office which she, as self-appointed janitor, was forever carrying around with her on her tours of inspection, and it also served, when turned end for end, as a quick if rather dry lunch, or something in the nature of a breakfast food. She would delicately snip the straws off it, one at a time, and holding them with one end in her mouth would push them slowly in, while the teeth, working at great speed, chopped it into tiny portions. This operation resembled the performance of a sword swallower, and the sound produced was similar to that of a sewing machine running a little out of control. A considerable dispute raged over this broom, but in the end I found it easier to buy new brooms and keep my mouth shut.

Occasionally she would be indisposed to come out of her apartment, and would hold long-winded conversations with me through the aperture in a sleepy voice, and this with rising and falling inflections, and a rhythm, that made it seem as though she was actually saying something, which perhaps she was. In fact her conversational proclivities were one of the highlights of this association, and her efforts to communicate with me in this manner were most expressive, and any remark addressed to my furry companion seldom failed to elicit a reply of some kind, when she was awake, and sometimes when she was asleep.

To fill her tank required daily five trips of water, and she got to know by the rattle of the pails when her water was to be changed. She would emerge from her seclusion and try to take an active part in the work, getting pretty generally in the way, and she insisted on pushing the door to between my trips, with a view to excluding the much dreaded current of cold air. This was highly inconvenient at times, but she seemed so mightily pleased with her attempts at cooperation that I made no attempt to interfere.

Certain things she knew to be forbidden she took a delight in doing, and on my approach her eyes would seem to kindle with a spark of unholy glee and she would scamper off squealing with trepidation, and no doubt well pleased at having put something over on me. Her self-assertive tendencies now began to be very noticeable. She commenced to take charge of the camp. She, so to speak, held the floor, also anything above it that was within her reach, by now a matter of perhaps two feet and more. This, as can be readily seen, included most of the ordinary fixtures. Fortunately, at this late season she had ceased her cutting operations, and was contented with pulling down anything she could lay her hands on, or climb up and get, upon which the article in question was subjected to a critical inspection as to its possibilities for inclusion into the rampart of heterogeneous objects that had been erected across her end of the camp, and behind which she passed from the entrance of her dwelling to the bathing pool. Certain objects such as the poker, a tin can, and a trap she disposed in special places, and if they were moved she would set them back in the positions she originally had for them, and would do this as often as they were removed. When working on some project she laboured with an almost fanatical zeal to the exclusion of all else, laying off at intervals to eat and comb her coat with the flexible double claw provided for that purpose.

She had the mischievous proclivities of a monkey, and she brightened many a dreary homecoming with her clumsy and frolicsome attempts at welcome. Headstrong past all belief, she had also the proprietary instinct natural to an animal, or a man, that builds houses and surrounds himself with works produced by his own labour. Considering the camp no doubt as her own personal property, she examined closely all visitors that entered it, some of whom on her account had journeyed from afar. Some passed muster, after being looked over in the most arrogant fashion, and were not molested; if not approved of, she would rear up against the legs of others, and try to push them over. This performance sometimes created a mild sensation, and gained for her the title of The Boss. Some ladies thought she should be called The Lady of the Lake, others The Queen. Jelly the Tub I called her, but the royal title stuck and a Queen she was, and ruled her little kingdom with no gentle hand.

There was one change that this lowly animal wrought in my habit of mind that was notable. Human companionship had always meant a lot to me. But before the coming of Anahareo I had enjoyed it only intermittently. Its place had been taken by those familiar objects with which I surrounded myself, which were a part of my life – a canoe, a pair of snowshoes that handled especially well, a thin-bladed, well-tempered hunting axe, an extra serviceable tump-line, my guns, a shrewdly balanced throwing knife. All these belongings had seemed like living things, almost, that could be depended on and that I carefully tended, that kept me company and that I was not above addressing on occasion. Now there was this supposedly dumb beast who had, if not entirely supplanted them, at least had relegated them to their normal sphere as useful pieces of equipment only. In this creature there was life and understanding; she moved and talked and did things, and gave me a response of which I had not thought an animal capable. She seemed to supply some need in my life of which I had been only dimly conscious heretofore, which had been growing with the years, and which marriage had for a time provided. And now that I was alone again it had returned, redoubled in intensity, and this sociable and home-loving beast, playful, industrious and articulate, fulfilled my yearning for companionship as no other creature save man, of my own kind especially, could ever have done. A dog, for all his affection and fidelity, was sometimes too utterly submissive. This creature comported itself as a person, of a kind, and she busied herself at tasks that I could, without loss of dignity, have occupied myself at; she made camp, procured and carried in supplies, could lay plans and carry them out and stood robustly and resolutely on her own hind legs, metaphorically and actually, and had an independence of spirit that measured up well with my own, seeming to look on me as a contemporary, accepting me as an equal and no more.

Her attempts at communication with me, sometimes ludicrous, often pitiful, and frequently quite understandable, as I got to know them, placed her, to my mind, high above the plane of ordinary beasts. This, and the community of interest we had of keeping things in shape, of keeping up the home so to speak, strengthened indissolubly the bond between the two of us, both creatures that were never meant to live alone.

Soon the snow was deep enough for good snow-shoeing, setting me free to cover the country easily and systematically, in an effort to establish definitely whether McGinnis and McGinty lived or not. All beavers found (to a hunter, even in the dead of winter, with three feet of snow on the ground, this is not so difficult as it would seem) could be easily re-located in the summer without waste of time, and their identity then ascertained. I found three more families, one of them within a few miles of the cabin and on the same waters. This latter discovery gave me no particular joy, as I had given up all idea of attempting any conservation project in a region where the inhabitants, on whose goodwill the safety of my protégés would depend, held animal life so cheaply. Any one of the several colonies could have been the retreat of the lost yearlings, but nothing could be determined about them till late summer, a beaver's habits being what they are.

I commenced to plan my book, but somehow was not able to get started. I had no idea how to put a book together. I bethought me of the 'Writing System' that Anahareo had brought away from her home thinking they were cookery books. I dug them out and soon became deeply absorbed in matters of Setting, Dialogue, Point of View, Unity of Impression, and Style. And while I could not put any of these instructions to their fullest use, having no very clear notion of what form, if any, my narrative would take, this 'Unity of Impression' that was so urgently recommended seemed to be of the first importance, and is the one point that since has kept my pen, a little inclined to wander into irrelevant bypaths of reminiscence, more or less within the limits of my subject. My stories seemed to have the peculiar faculty of writing themselves and they generally ended up in an entirely different direction from what they started in, so that the forepart had to be completely re-arranged to satisfy this exacting and at times exceedingly troublesome rule.

Meantime, I could not but worry about Anahareo, although she was well equipped and under the care of a man whose equal as a woodsman was seldom to be met, for I knew the country they had gone into, a region of very large lakes and severe storms, and having a climate that made winter in Temiscouata seem like late Fall weather by comparison.

With these thoughts on my mind I found it impossible to concentrate. Thinking that a visit to the scene of our earlier struggles, and that the atmosphere of the place where my first literary aspirations had been born, might be something in the nature of an inspiration, I gave my camp into the care of a friend, and loading my toboggan with a light outfit made the long pilgrimage to Birch Lake.

On arrival I made camp at the same old tenting ground, using even the same poles, that had been so carefully laid by for future use.

The place was sadly changed. Though the roofing was torn and the chinking had mostly fallen out, the camp was otherwise much as we had left it. But the beaver dam had gone out of repair and the lake, once the snow was off it, would be little better than a rock-studded swamp. The beaver house, untenanted, stood high above the empty basin, the entrance plainly visible. Even the muskrats must have left there long ago. The birds were all gone and a stranger squirrel scurried away at my approach. But the great pines still stood towering, mighty in their silence.

My feelings as I entered the cabin were those of one who visits a shrine. The relics were all there, though the now leaky roof had afforded small protection to them. The famous war-bonnet hung limp and lifeless, its gay feathers bedraggled, and the warrior, the Sign of Welcome gone from off his face, was but a wooden block. The homely paintings, that had looked so like beadwork if you stood away from them a little, were marred and disfigured, and partly washed away. The Christmas tree leaned dry and withered where we had left it, in its corner. The cut table-legs, the chewed deerskins, and drinking dish upon the floor, the very tooth marks — Anahareo's curtains on the windows, all were there. The redoubt built with such pathetic industry remained intact, but no small black eyes peered wisely through the peep-hole in the end of it, no gambolling elfin figures raced from behind it in mock battle, no small wailing voices declaimed aloud.

I took my old place sadly on the bench and wished I had not come. And as I sat in reverie it fell to dusk. But outside the sky was still crimson from the sunset, and the glow from it shone redly through the gaping crevices and was reflected down the vacant stove pipe hole, so that the floor and walls were coloured with it. And the dingy, empty cabin was transformed, and took on again something of the glamour of its former days, and seemed once more an enchanted hall of dreams. So that it was no more an abandoned heap of logs and relics, but was once again the House of McGinnis in all its former glory. .

And quite suddenly the place that had seemed to be so lonely and deserted was now no longer empty, but all at once was filled with living memories and ghosts from out the past. And then I made a light, and here amongst the wraiths began to write.

In two nights, two chapters of *The Vanishing Frontier*[1] were finished: 'The Tale of the Beaver People', and 'The House of McGinnis'. I made out in my writing that our lost friends still were living. And they lived again in those few pages if nowhere else.

For a week I wrote furiously, while ever in my ears was the soft laughter of a woman, and the sound of small voices that were so much like the voices of little children. And the phantoms sat with me and moved and played, and the characters in my stories lived again. And they were not sad, these wraiths of yesterday, but happy ones, and walked in gladness before me as I wrote. And I found myself able, at last, to capture thoughts that had hitherto been beyond expression. And here it was borne upon me why they had so much impressed themselves upon us, these little beasts. They had been like little Indians in their ways, and had seemed emblematic of the race, a living link with our environment, a living breathing manifestation of that elusive Something, that Spirit of the Waste Lands that so permeated our own lives, that had existed always just beyond our reach, and could never before be grasped in its entirety. In some tangible way they and their kind typified the principle that is inherent in all Nature. The animal supreme of all the forest, they were the Wilderness personified, the Wild articulate, the Wild that was our home, and still lived embodied in the warp and woof of it. Through them I had a new conception of Nature. Although I had not hitherto given the matter much consideration, it was not inconceivable that every other creature, and perhaps every other thing was, according to its place and use,

1. The title was changed by the publishers to *Men of the Last Frontier*.

as well provided to fulfil its special purpose as were they, though not perhaps so obviously. I had lived with Nature all my life, yet had never felt so close to it before, as I better understood the Spirit that had fashioned it — nor yet so far a part from it, in the sudden knowledge of my own unfitness to interpret or describe it. As well now attempt a history of the Creation.

So I kept my theme well within the limits of personal observation and experience, and left interpretation to those of greater skill in writing.

The swing of an Indian on snowshoes, the rolling, easy gait of a bear, the lightly undulating progress of a swift canoe, the black sweeping rush of water at the head of a falls, the slow swaying of the tree-tops, were all words from the same script, strokes from the same brush, each a resonance from the changeless rhythm that rocks the Universe. We were more kin to those creatures than we had known.

My writing even had sprung from these things, they ran all through it. And I sorrowed no more. The tree falls and nourishes another. From death springs life; it is the Law. And these writings that were no longer mine, but which I now saw only as recorded echoes and not creations of my own, had captured, in their poor way, the essentials of what had eluded me so long.

And I felt at last that I had been made to understand. And the house of McGinnis, as I left it in the starlight, seemed no longer a headstone at the grave of lost hopes, was no more an end, but a beginning. And before leaving I took one or two peeled sticks and some chips, a few brown hairs, and a dried sprig from off the Christmas tree, and rolled them tightly in a piece of buckskin, to be my medicine, my luck, and for a token.

And I bid the cheerful ghosts farewell and left them

there behind me; yet as I journeyed onwards down the well-remembered trail, whereon no tracks showed in the starlight save my own, I felt that in the darkness there behind me was a woman, and with her two little beavers in a stove.

3

The coming of Rawhide

On arriving home I was presented by my friend with another letter from Anahareo. The possibility of hearing from her by air mail never had occurred to me. They were safe and well, but Dave's claim had been staked just twenty-eight days before their arrival, and was rated the richest property in the whole area. They had both had to work for wages on what was to have been their gold mine. Dave's last Eldorado was gone; and he was old. Broken and embittered, he had gone out, back to his own land to lay his bones with those of his fathers, beneath the singing pine trees on the Ottawa. Anahareo was waiting for the break-up in order to return. This would not be till early June.

So now the book was no longer a pastime but a serious undertaking; on the proceeds of this venture we must depend to make a move, and we got right busy, Jelly and I. From then on I worked unremittingly on my script, writing at night and going out only to replenish the wood supply. I did not, and do not, aim at literary excellence, it being beyond me, sacrificing what might be correct usage to paint a picture in words. I felt, and still feel, that if I had to pay too much attention to technical niceties, my thoughts might be dressed in a coat of mail, rather than in the softer habiliments with which Nature clothes even her grimmest realities. If I considered that by putting a word in front that should be behind, and *vice versa*, I could better express some thought, I would do so, on the same principle whereby a snowshoe is often handier to dig snow with than a shovel. My factory-made English on which I had looked with something approaching contempt, could now be put to some use. It was brought out of cold storage where it had languished for the better part of three decades, and on inspection, in the light of modern requirements, was found to be woefully short on words. This had to be mended, and I wrestled for hours with books of reference on the English language. From a book of English poems, Longfellow's *Hiawatha*, and Service's *Songs of a Sourdough* I unearthed verses suggestive of the chapters they introduced, a fashion long out of date, it was said, but it appealed to me and I was not interested in fashions; I was getting something off my chest.

The pile of MS. increased to imposing and rather alarming proportions. I often awoke from sleep to make alterations, made constant notes, and to get the proper effect of difficult passages, I read them aloud to Jelly, who, pleased with the attention and the sound of rattling papers, would twist and turn in queer contortions of delight. I erected a table alongside the bunk, so that I could sit there and reach out at any moment and jot down any notions that came along.

And while I wrote Jelly pursued her own studies, and carried on with her highly important jobs such as moving and placing objects, and took care of little household chores such as banking up the bottom of the door, or the re-arrangement of the wood pile. Often she would sit bolt upright beside me on the bed, looking up in a most intent manner at my face, as though trying to fathom what my purpose could be with that queer scratching noise. She was a paper addict and was much attracted by the rustle of the stationery, and constantly stole wrapping paper and magazines and books, taking them home with her. When she was on the bunk with me she would reach out very often at my note-book and other papers, and we sometimes had lively discussions on this matter in which I was not always the winner.

One day however she succeeded, quite, I think, beyond her expectations or mine. Forgetting to erect the barrier between the bunk and the table, I returned from cutting wood one day to find everything pushed off it, including a camera, a lamp, and a row of books; and she had registered her entire approval of my literary efforts by removing the MS. bodily. A few sheets of my work were scattered on the floor, but the rest were not to be seen. A visit of investigation to the abode of the culprit was received with squeals of mingled trepidation and protest, but I routed her out and raked up the manuscript with the blackened wooden poker and a piece of wire, the paper fiend meanwhile trying desperately to maintain her rights of ownership. Luckily all of it but one page was recovered, and as she had no doubt scooped up the entire pile with that steam shovel of a bottom jaw of hers, it was little damaged. But the resulting mix-up was very little short of cataclysmic. Imagine about four hundred loose sheets closely written on both sides, in pencil, with interpolations, alterations, and notes wedged in here and there, with lines and arrows and other cabalistic indications of what went where, and *unnumbered*, and you may get the idea. It took me the best part of three days to reassemble, and in some instances, rewrite the script. This time I painstakingly numbered the pages.

So we kept on with our book, Jelly and I, and it began to draw to a close. And I wrote not so much of men, whose comings and goings, whose very existence, was of such small significance in the vastness of the Great White

Silence, but of the Frontier in all its aspects and its phases, the Frontier that even now was vanishing, seemed indeed to be already gone; for the ruins amongst which I now was living showed only too plainly what its fate was soon to be.

Came Christmas, which we two spent together. I think Jelly enjoyed it, as she ate so much that she was in visible discomfort all the next day, but my own lone festivities were rather futile and a little unhappy. However, I hung up a paper lantern from a rafter and after the candle in it was lighted Jelly did happen to look up at it a couple of times, so I didn't feel so flat and ridiculous about it after all. I had several invitations for New Year's, and leaving Jelly well fixed for water and feed, and the camp well warmed, I spent that afternoon and night in Cabano.

On this holiday the French Canadian throws himself into the spirit of joyous conviviality of the season with a carefree abandon that throws wide all doors, opens all hearts, and puts a period to all feuds; and he allows, on this day of the year, this *Jour de l'an*, his robust love of merriment to have full sway.

In town everything had a festive air. The streets were full of people dressed in all their best. Church bells were ringing, men arrived hourly from the woods in strings, singing as they passed along the streets, and the whole village had such an atmosphere of goodwill and bonhomie bubbling up from it, that no weather however stormy or evil could possibly have penetrated or subdued it, if indeed it would ever have been noticed. Music could be heard in every direction, from the organized revelry of the radio, to the blare of a gramophone, and there issued out upon the frosty air the skirl of fiddles, playing the wild rhythms of the jigs and reels and the clever and intricate step dances in which these people find an outlet for their feelings which is peculiarly their own.

There seemed something so very reminiscent of the intimate community spirit of an Indian village in all of it, that a wave of homesickness swept over me as I passed down the narrow tree-lined streets. But this was soon driven entirely from my mind as I was saluted on all sides, shaken by the hand, and called into houses that I had never before entered, and made to partake of whatever cheer they were all enjoying. And it was all done in such an unpretentious, genuine, and simple way that I clean forgot that I was a gloomy half-breed, and gave my best in entertainment in return.

Every house was full of music and play and laughter. Here were no funereal, stupifying 'rhythms' or erotic, maudlin inanities, but gay quadrilles, fine old waltzes, snappy fox-trots; and whatever the circumstances of the host, whether he laid a ceremonious feast, or could afford no more than fried pork or venison or good French bread, the parting guest was sped with a full belly and good wishes, and perhaps a few glasses of red wine to fortify him against his journey home.

And at midnight a fusillade of shots was fired from every kind of firearm, and timed by every kind of clock, so that volleys were being fired from time to time for several minutes, according to whether clocks were fast or slow. And as long as the bullets were sent up and out in the general direction of the lake no one cared a great deal where they fell, as no good citizen had any business to be outside the town on such a night.

In the midst of all the celebration and the merriment I thought suddenly of my little brown buddy, waiting up there alone in the dark and empty cabin in the hills. So I slipped away on my snowshoes through the midnight forest to my home behind the Mountain of the Elephant; and with a parcel of peanuts and apples and candies, Jelly had her New Year's too, and enjoyed it every bit as much as I had done – better perhaps, because she had no memories behind her.

Late in February I sent the completed MS. away, and being now free I commenced the study of words, with the assistance of my book of synonyms and a dictionary. I found words elusive and hard to trap. But each one as it was cornered up in a book or magazine was caught, and went down into a note-book and was brought home and given a thorough and exhaustive going over. Often it would have little to recommend it save that I liked the sound of it. I sought words that suggested in their pronunciation the idea I would try to express by means of them. I became vocabulary-conscious, began to use four and five dollar words, and often my conversation was unintelligible even to my English-speaking friends. I had attacks of absent mindedness, and eventually got to the stage where I once reached for the ink bottle to fill my pipe, and another time caught myself on the point of attempting to fill my pen out of the tobacco can. Progress by any other name could have been no worse.

There was a lawyer who often visited me, always bringing cheer with him, and sometimes a merry crowd of friends. He seldom came without some gift for me and once showed up in the middle of the night, having lost his way, and announced that he had left a radio down the trail a piece. It was a portable model, and the next day we packed it in, with its appurtenances. This machine was a complete mystery to me, but he installed it and rigged the aerial, and that night the camp, usually so quiet, was filled with music.

I overcame my aversion to any form of machinery, from ploughs to railroads, sufficiently well to listen in on this set. Here, I soon discovered, was a word-mine all by itself. From then on radio announcers, authors, book reviewers, news reporters, politicians, and others whose trade is words, became my nightly company. These people and the works of Emerson and Shakespeare, and the Bible, each made their unwitting contribution to my omnivorous appetite for the means wherewith to express myself.

Always, night-travelling had had an irresistible fascination for me. This familiarity with darkness and the development of certain faculties that went with it, stood me in good stead in my work of patrolling and in locating Jelly at any and all hours; and between tours on the rounds of my self imposed duties, and at intervals between sleeps, I studied the English language from dark to sunrise. My coal oil bill went up, and the books I bought cut deeply into my eating money; but there were lots of deer and for clothes I wore buckskin, taking time out to tan the hides. This latter practice attracted the attention of the local game warden, who came in armed with written orders to impose a fine on me. I had to talk pretty fast to him to get him to see things my way, and saying that he felt there had been a mistake he advised me to write to Quebec City. This I did, and later received from the head warden of the district, a letter expressing regret for the trouble I had been put to, and a hunting and trapping licence was awarded me free of charge. Again the noblesse of Old Quebec.

During the New Year's festivities I had become acquainted with an Irish family who all but adopted me, using me as though I had been son and brother, giving me the freedom of their home. A carefree happy-go-lucky group of people they were, who cared little whether I wore my hat backwards, sideways, or at all, and who made my coming the signal for a gay party of music and singing. And with them I formed a friendship that exists today, and at this distance, as strong as ever it was then. It was after one of these visits that I returned on a day late in March, to find the camp door open and my little companion of a lonely winter gone.

I stared stupidly at the open door: my head swam for a moment with the sudden, devastating feeling of bereavement, and I remember that I shouted once aloud, made some meaningless sounds. Then I got busy. At first I thought she had been taken, but evidently she had at last solved the problem of opening the door from the inside having long learned the trick of shutting it. The warm sun of an early spring afternoon had lured her out to a not improbable death by freezing, as there was as yet no open water and there was easily four feet of snow in the bush. Her tracks revealed that she had been gone a full day, and her trail led up the lake to her playhouse of the Fall before.

Unable to find an opening in the ice she had followed the course of the creek upstream, and at no place did it offer a chance of entry. The stream eventually petered out in a maze of alders and cedar swamp in which she had wandered in all directions. She penetrated this swamp for a distance of about a mile and then became lost entirely, digging deeply into the snow in spots, in a futile endeavour to find water. Her steps were becoming short, and in many places she had lain down for long periods thawing out a bed for herself. It was easy to see where night had caught her, as a crust had then commenced to form, on which she left less and less impression as it hardened; and the poor ugly in-toed tracks became indistinct and finally disappeared altogether – and still headed away from home and safety. The temperature had abruptly dropped and a beaver's feet and tail freeze easily, completely disabling him.

I did not return to camp that night but hunted the swamp till daylight, calling every few minutes. I searched it and the surrounding gullies and ravines in all directions, that day and many succeeding days, and there being a moon, for as many nights as it lasted. Came a spell of almost zero weather, not infrequent during early spring. I then knew that if my little chum had by any series of accidents escaped the foxes and was still without sufficient water, she would be by now almost certainly frozen to death; and in support of this theory I one day found a porcupine in that condition.

The weather later became soft and I travelled day after day combing the country for signs of the wanderer, even visiting lakes to which she probably could never have got. At the end of twenty days I sat dispirited and well nigh worn out from dragging heavy snowshoes over wet snow at a time of year when bush travelling is considered virtually impossible. My injured foot had given out and my snowshoes were so worn as to be almost useless, but as there had been a couple of days of heavy rain followed by a sharp frost, I decided to take advantage of the crust that formed and make one more attempt. I repaired my snowshoes as best I could and was starting out, when I saw a black object working its way along the shore line, about fifty yards away and headed for the cabin. For a moment I watched it, and then, the certainty entering my mind that my search was ended, I went forward and met it and there, plodding slowly but persistently ahead, poor as a rake and otherwise the worse for wear, came my long lost friend the Boss.

It was a great reunion. For her part, she took up camp life about where she had laid it down, had a good feed, slept for twenty-four hours, and said no more about it. I later found where her unerring instinct had located water in the nearly dry bed of the stream, and she had holed up there for nearly three weeks, under the snow, until the rain had created a freshet on which she had descended to the lake, and there being by then a strip of open water she had been released.

Come open water she left the camp, and I much feared that she would leave on some rambling excursion to look for a partner, and finding one, not return. But she waived her privilege and proceeded up the lake, where she formally took up her abode in her burrow, visiting me regularly several times a night. She followed the canoe around the lake and surprised me one day by scrambling over the side and flopping into it. This seemed at the time a little extraordinary, and especially remarkable was her manner of doing this, as she had a nice sense of equilibrium, canting the canoe only a few inches. She continued this practice, and varied the performance by climbing on to the stern seat and taking a high dive into the lake, slipping smoothly into the water as though oiled.

On what I took to be special occasions she played a kind of a game with me, giving me a false lead as to her intended direction, and then diving. I would attempt to follow her, and she would suddenly appear in a totally unexpected spot some distance away. On my approach she would birl round and round like a log, or spin in an erect position, partly out of the water, and throw herself backwards with a mighty splash in very evident pleasure, perhaps at having fooled me. This she would do for perhaps half an hour at a time. She would sometimes dive alongside the canoe, and I could see her straining every muscle to gain on me while supposedly out of sight, and on coming to the surface ahead of the canoe, which of course I always made sure to allow for, she would wait for me to catch up and then repeat.

She often signalled me by calling, giving a clear penetrating note capable of being heard for half a mile, and
should I call her with a similar sound she seldom failed to
answer me, if within earshot. Her favourite amusement
was to place her two front legs around my wrist, gripping
hard, and standing erect with my hand pressing against
her breast, she would push and strain in a sustained effort
to upset me. Sometimes in the course of this pastime she
would back up, trying to drag me forward until I was off
balance and then attempt to rush me off my feet. She now
weighed all of twenty pounds and was solid bone and
muscle, and was surprisingly strong. I have since found
that there was nothing very out of the ordinary in these
activities as they are all customary amusements of any
beaver; the remarkable part is, that she should elect to remain with me and so employ herself, instead of seeking
her own kind of which there was a colony less than three
miles away, and easily accessible to her.

Just before the leaves came I set a trap for a marauding
otter, on a stream some distance away, as I had found
beaver hair in his droppings; Jelly, on account of her op-
timistic outlook on life, would fall an easy victim. One
morning on visiting the trap I found it gone, and project-
ing from under a submerged log saw the tail of a beaver.
On pulling the chain I found resistance, and hauled out a
living beaver, an adult. He had a piece of his scalp hanging
loose, and half-drowned and scared almost to death, he
made little attempt to defend himself. I removed the trap
and took him home with me, tied up in a gunny sack. His
foot was badly injured, and being one of the all-important
hind, or swimming feet, I decided to try and repair the
damage before I liberated him. For the first twenty-four
hours he hid himself in the Boss's late apartment, emerging only to drink, and he ate not at all. At the end of that

time he came out into the centre of the camp with every appearance of fear, but I was able to pick him up and speaking kindly to him, offered him an apple which he took. I worked on him all night doing my best to inspire confidence, and succeeded to the extent that, crippled as he was, he commenced a tour of the camp, examining everything including the door, which he made no attempt to bite through. In the course of his explorations he discovered the bunk, climbed into it up Jelly's chute, found it to his liking, and from then on ate and slept there, occasionally leaving it for purposes of his own, such as to dispose of his peeled sticks or to take a bath. He slept between my pillow and the wall, and nearly every night he became lonesome and came around to sleep in the crook of my arm till daylight, when he went back behind the pillow. I might add here that I was under no hardship, as a beaver is perhaps one of the cleanest animals in existence. After all I was responsible for his condition, and any small sacrifices that I had to make were cheerfully submitted to.

Although the weather was still cold I dared light no fire in the camp, as the noise of the stove drove him frantic; tobacco smoke caused him to hide away for hours. The operation of dressing his foot single handed was an undertaking of no mean proportions. It was swollen to an immense size, and two of the metatarsal bones projected through the skin. His teeth were badly shattered from his attempts to break the trap, and it would be weeks before they were again serviceable. The loose portion of his scalp had dried, and hung from his head like a piece of wrinkled hide, so I severed it and named him after it, calling him Rawhide, a name he still retains and knows.

For two weeks I worked hard to save the injured foot, and to a certain extent succeeded, although I believe the antiseptic effect of the leeches which clustered in the wound on his subsequent return to natural conditions, completed a task that taxed my ingenuity to the utmost. Whether on account of the attention he received, or because labouring under the impression that I had saved his life, or from very lonesomeness, I cannot say, but the poor creature took a liking to me, hobbling around the camp at my heels, and crying out loudly in the most mournful fashion when I went out.

These sounds on one occasion attracted the attention of the Boss who raced up to ascertain the cause. On seeing a strange beaver she nearly broke her neck trying to get out of the camp, running in her haste full tilt into the door, which I had closed. She then reconsidered the matter, and returned to give the newcomer the once over. She at once decided that here was somebody who, being disabled, would be perfectly easy to beat up, which kind and chivalrous thought she immediately proceeded to put into execution. After a considerable scramble which ended in my having to carry the would-be warrior bodily down to the lake, objecting loudly, quiet was restored. She apparently resented the presence of a stranger in the home, no matter whose home; she ruled here as queen and had no intention of sharing her throne with anybody, it seemed, and I had to fasten the door from then on to keep her out.

On my patient becoming convalescent I bid him good luck and turned him loose, not without some feelings of regret, as he had become very likeable and affectionate. The next day, on visiting the domicile of the so-militant Queen, I saw a beaver and called it over. The animal answered and swam towards me, and my surprise can be well imagined, when I recognized the now well known voice and lines of the cripple. He came to the canoe with every sign of recognition, followed me down the full length of the lake, and crept behind me into the camp.

While there he lay for a time on a deerskin rug, and whimpered a little and nibbled gently at my hands, and presently slipped away to the lake again. And this practice he continued, sometimes climbing, with assistance, on to my knees and there conducting an assiduous and very damp toilet. He had nothing to gain by these manoeuvres, and could have left at any time for parts unknown, had he been so minded.

While I cannot go so far as to say that he was grateful, there is little doubt but that the treatment he had received while sick and confined to the cabin had had its effect on him, for he haunted me and the camp environs, unless driven away by the Boss, whose treatment of him was little short of brutal. She was insanely jealous and drove him away from the camp repeatedly, and would not allow him to approach me if she were present. On more than one occasion she chased him far down the stream below the outlet, where I could hear him crying out; but he always stuck to his guns and came back. In spite of her hostility he followed her around and did everything she did, hobbling on his injured foot emitting plaintive little sounds, and seeming almost pitifully anxious to fit into the picture and be one of the boys. He even succeeded, after several failures, in climbing into the canoe, only to be thrown out by the Boss, on which I interfered. He somehow gave the impression that he was starving for companionship, and Jelly refusing his advances he turned to me. He did all these unaccustomed things in such a dumb and humble way, yet with such an air of quiet resolution about him, that I always took his part against the more flamboyant and self-sufficient Jelly Roll. And by this very quiet insistence, this exercise of some unexpected latent power within him, he overcame one by one the obstacles imposed on him by his new environment and found his place at last, and eventually took control and became no more a suppliant but a leader.

The Boss had for me the friendship that exists between equals; we were rough and tumble play-fellows, old-timers together who could take liberties with one another and get away with it. Rawhide seemed to want only a little kindness to make him happy, and was as gentle as the touch of the night wind on the leaves; yet I once saw him, driven to passion by too much persecution, shake the Boss like she had been a paper bag.

And I think she owes it to him that she lives today.

A rogue beaver, old and watchful and wise, his colony no doubt destroyed by hunters, descended on these two while I was away and tried to take possession. On my return I found Jelly laid out on the landing before the camp. A thin trail of blood led to the door but she must have been too weak to enter, and had dragged herself back to the water's edge to wait. Her throat was torn open, some of the parts protruding; her bottom lip was nearly severed, both arms were punctured and swollen and nearly useless, and her tail had been cut completely through at the root for over an inch of its width and there were besides a number of ugly gashes on the head and body. There was nothing I could do save to disinfect the wounds. Meanwhile she lay inert, her eyes closed, moaning faintly, while her blood oozed away into the mud of the landing she had so stoutly maintained as her own; and in her extremity she had come to me, her friend, who could only sit helplessly by, resolving to let her quietly die beside her pond.

I sat beside her all night, and at intervals fed her milk with the old glass syringe that once before had brought her back from the edge of the Valley of Shadows. Towards morning she seemed to draw on some hidden resources of vitality and bestirred herself, and slowly, painfully, crawled up into the cabin; for I did not dare to pick her up for fear of opening up her now clotted wounds afresh. She stayed with me all that day, leaving again at night, in bad shape but with the best part of two cans of milk inside her, and apparently on the mend. Only the marvellous recuperative powers possessed by wild animals and man in a state of nature, brought her around. I did not see her again for a week, but often passed the time of day with her through the walls of her abode, and heard her answer me. By the signs I discovered around the lake and from what I saw of him another time, the visitor must have been of enormous size, and there is no doubt that had she been alone she would have been killed. Rawhide also bore marks of the encounter but to a less degree, and I am sure by what I have since seen of his other abilities, that his assistance must have turned the tide of battle.

From then on the two of them lived in perfect harmony, and have done ever since. But with the knowledge that the presence of an intruder may result in pain and suffering, to her all strangers, human or animal, from then on were anathema. Guests who wished to view the beavers might no longer stand on the recognized landing places or trails and admire the beauty of the fur, the intelligence of the eye, the noble lines of the head, and so forth. They, the guests, were firmly and none too politely pushed off the said trail or landing. The shore, the lake itself, the canoe, she claimed them all. Even the camp, it appeared, was hers, as she chased people out of it and ran them up the road, and it was highly probable that she even thought she built it.

They both acted much as if they owned the pond and environs, and certainly without them it would have been just a shallow, lifeless, muddy sheet of water. Their presence there gave life to it, and imparted to the valley an indefinable air of being occupied that no other creature save man could give to it. Many came to this hitherto deserted spot because of them, and it became something of a metropolis, in a mild way of speaking. And some of those who came, with the poetic instinct of the Frenchman, thought it should be named for them, and so the hills that trooped down from the crest of high Elephant Mountain and stood gathered around the lake, became the Jelly Roll Hills and the pond was Rawhide Lake; and knowing well the history of the camp they named it Beaver's Home.

So we were all officially designated on the local records, and all three of us proved up on our possession by improving the estate. The beavers cleaned out runways and landings in convenient places, and built a lodge and kept the dam ship-shape and up to date, while I banked my own cabin and re-chinked it, and brightened up the interior a little and raked the yard.

Near their house the beavers cleared themselves a playground, on which no human being but myself might set a foot, and Jelly once chased a party of three people off this place, two of whom retired to high ground and another climbed a tree.

And the Queen deliberately stood up in the centre of her plaza, and shook and twisted her head and body in the irresistibly mirth-provoking contortions with which a beaver shows his appreciation of what he considers to be a very good joke.

A beaver's memory is long, and I think she has never quite forgotten that adventure that so nearly cost her life, and even today, if I be absent, the Queen will tolerate no stranger on the place.

4

The Dark Hour and the Dawn

IN early August, at which time beavers are localized in their permanent works, I took up again my quest, the only thing that was keeping me in this cut and tortured remnant of a wilderness with its ever present menace to the lives of my two dependents. There was little food for them on the shores of the pond and once it was exhausted they might leave me; one more year in this locality would make a move imperative, though I was well aware that no matter where I went every man's hand would be against them, and that I might some day be forced into serious trouble on their account. Every time I received a cheque for an article I was sorely tempted to abandon my hopeless search, leave someone in charge of the beavers, and make a journey back to Ontario and find some point where we would all have a safer and more congenial environment. But I quenched these disloyal thoughts. I quit writing entirely, having run out of material and unable, between trips, to apply the concentration necessary to the elaboration of new themes. So I gave up all thoughts of literary work in the prosecution of my hunt.

A month's travel proved beyond any doubt that none of the few scattered lodges and bank dens previously located were occupied by McGinnis and McGinty. Some of the townspeople took a lively interest in the affair, and I received much well-meant information. But it takes a hunter to read the signs with any accuracy, and these clues rarely amounted to anything. But I followed them every one to the end, travelling through swamps and slash, sleeping out in any weather only to find, after days of wandering, an old lodge that had been deserted for years, or more frequently the cuttings of a porcupine instead of those of beavers.

This search had lost its reality to me, and had become an uncompleted mission which must be adhered to from a sense of duty, until every chance had been eliminated, in the possibility, but no longer the expectation, of its fulfilment. And when with an empty belly, sometimes in the darkness, often in the rain, perhaps after dragging for miles through tangled, mosquito-infested cedar swamps in which it was at times necessary to crawl, I pursued some phantom clue to its inevitable failure, it assumed the proportions of a nightmare in which one struggles hopelessly to gain some vital but unattainable goal. The all-too-evident hopelessness of my object, now no longer to be disguised, together with a number of other things, weighed heavily on my mind. It was long since I had heard from Anahareo; not only was she far removed from any means of communication, but she herself would not return for months. The mine on which we had so depended had failed us, and unable to get out of the country she might become destitute among strangers. Our sole income was my small pension; there was no work to be had here, and if there had been I could not have taken it without leaving the beavers unprotected. I was alone in what amounted to a foreign land, and there was moreover the depressing influence, exceedingly potent, of the country itself, this terrible graveyard of a blasted ruined forest, slashed, racked and slaughtered, a wilderness with the soul torn out of it. These factors and the ever present danger to the beavers were ever before me. There seemed to be no way out.

Added to this, M. Duchene, my lawyer friend, had died, leaving behind him a sense of deprivation and a real regret. Even the beavers had taken to him. During the summer when both beavers were frequenting the camp, he had stayed several nights. He slept in the bunk alone while I lay on the floor, as I frequently did. The first morning, on waking, I asked him how he had slept and he said not too well. On being asked the reason, he said that he had no room in the bed. 'Look,' he told me; and there in the bunk with him, stretched out on their backs and occupying most of the bed, lay the two beavers fast asleep!

Had these animals, to whom strangers were always an object of indifference, if not actual suspicion, been able to so decipher the generous character of this man? I wondered. He never knew just what his gift of a radio had meant to me, and for a long time I left it silent on its box.

On the shores of one pond on which lived two beavers whose identity I had not yet established, I once found a bed of brush; beside it were some empty rifle shells, and carefully wrapped up and concealed, a powerful jacklight. The hunters would evidently return. Taking a position directly across the narrow sheet of water, just behind the low ridge that bordered it, I lay in waiting four days and five nights, living on snared rabbits broiled before the embers of careful smokeless fires. On the fifth afternoon the hunters came. I appeared suddenly and without sound behind them, armed. The moral effect was quite good. However, it transpired that I knew these men and believed they were what they claimed themselves to be – poor devils out of a job, trying to get some meat for their families. Pot-hunters, if you will, but who had a better right than they? They were even unaware of the presence here of beavers. But I requested them to move, making no mention of the illegal jack-light which was none of my business, unless they had been obstinate. I took them to a good deer-lick; perhaps they had some luck there.

But things were not always so smooth. Nevertheless I had my way, always, as fortune had it, by fair means; in emergency I would have not been particular as to the means. I could understand better the old-time Indian's point of view, the atrocities they committed in defence of their families and homes, or to safeguard a piece of territory, an individual tree, a shrine, or a rock. Some hostility was aroused. It was said by some that I did not, according to law, possess any beavers, that they belonged to the province; to them it was a question of ownership, chattels, law. We own no lives but our own and I sought only to save, if possible, two that I valued.

That I should make enemies was inevitable, and incidents occurred that are best not recorded. And many miles from home, sometimes with camp made or even waking from sleep, I would suddenly become obsessed by the thought that the volunteer assistant who took charge of my little community in my absence had become tired of his thankless task, and had left Jelly and Rawhide open to attack from some ill-wisher; and I would hurry homeward day and night through the tangled slash. But my faithful friend was always at his post, nor did he ever give any sign of impatience, although the pickings were often pretty thin at Rawhide Lake, as I was now living on my infinitesimal army pension. Eggs, caviare and champagne entered the cabin only by way of the loud speaker, and the beavers too went pretty short on treats. They always begged for them, and when after buying only absolute necessaries for myself there remained a few dimes and nickels, these were always invested in a parcel of apples. And the little beasts were so overjoyed to have them, and it was so much pleasure to witness their enjoyment, that

I found it no hardship to stint myself the least bit in tobacco and some other things that were not real necessities, so as not to disappoint them too often.

I received another letter from Anahareo. With the wages she had earned driving a dog team all the previous winter for a company, she had bought herself a grubstake, and was on the trail of another fortune. This was probably for the best, as although her presence here on patrol in my stead would have set me free to go to work, if any such was to be had here, yet the deadly monotony of the place would in time have been very depressing, and perhaps have driven her away again. If only I could present her with McGinnis and McGinty on her return, the loss of the gold mine would be of small account!

Meanwhile, with the intensive observations I took, and experiments I conducted to ascertain the movements and identity of any beavers that came within the wide orbit of my reconnoitring, I was accumulating more and more data concerning these animals than I had considered possible; and my previous knowledge was as nothing compared with what I now commenced to learn. I found that by the exercise of a little patience and judgement I could, in course of time, get to see different members of a family within a measurable distance, provided they were house beaver and not individuals living in a bank. After my familiarity with my own animals, it seemed only natural that I should be able to confidently approach any and all of them, even if wild, and it's probable that three years of living on the closest terms with these creatures must have had its unconscious influence on my conduct and manner of approach.

Even my very attitude of mind may have communicated itself to them, as animals seem gifted that way. I found that, after some days of quiet watchfulness, I could inspire these elusive creatures with some measure of confidence, and that at the sound of my voice, not in imitation of their own calls but in tones of a certain pitch, they would sometimes leave their house and swim back and forth or lie quietly on the water, observing me, at a distance of a few yards. One, a young fellow, actually came ashore and peeled a stick, disregarding me utterly, and could have been no more than six feet away. There was nothing supernatural in all this, and I think that any other person who had had the same acquaintance with them, and who felt about them as I did, could have had the same experience. I believe that animals having a high mentality, and that have not suffered at the hands of man will, if given an opportunity, come to a conclusion regarding his intention towards them and act accordingly. Interesting as these experiments were, I eventually desisted from them, as the beavers would fall a prey to the hunters soon enough, without my dulling their instincts of self-protection for my own gratification.

The two that were now my sole company were, in the fearless intimacy of their relations with me, adding to my store of information daily. I saw them continuously, and within touching distance, occupied in all the arts of their profession, adding their quota of interest to what was to be the most eventful summer of my career. These two were completing a house and dam. And never before having had the same opportunity of seeing these erections in process of actual construction to such advantage, I spent hours watching them. My advent was always a signal to knock off work for the purpose of playing a wet, splashy kind of game, and this occurred at intervals all night; but the greater part of the time was spent in labour that was never abandoned till after daylight.

The interest inspired by their activities would alone

have caused me to spend the night watches in this manner, but this was also made advisable by the presence of the numbers of poachers and would-be hunters that ranged the woods, and these would be a menace from now until the beavers were safely ensconced in the camp. For I did not intend them to pass the winter in their new house half a mile away, owing to the danger of their being trapped some day while I slept. But they had made elaborate preparations and were every day adding to them, and in their search for material they stole every movable article they could find and utilized it in some manner or another.

One night the paddles were removed from the canoe, to be found later firmly enmeshed in the structure of the house. This edifice, besides the usual material of sticks and mud, had sometimes a weird assortment of household articles embedded in its surface like raisins in a pudding, all of which had to be surreptitiously extracted. Bones, bottles, firewood and old bags were taken and utilized in the building of the dam, and I returned once from town to be greeted at the landing by a pile of objects of a very varied description, including a shovel, a bag containing potatoes, a box of foolscap, a pair of pants and a catalogue, and interspersed through this collection were numerous blocks of stove wood. Other materials lay scattered along the trail in various stages of transportation, all destined for the lodge and dam. I had left the camp door secured against them, but these ambulating saw-mills had easily gained entrance by simply carving away a portion of the door. The good work was still going on when I arrived, and I was met with great acclaim and much excited rolling and falling on backs, and they seemed mightily pleased with themselves.

On yet another occasion I entered the cabin to find Jelly on the bunk busily engaged in ripping up and pushing overboard my carefully laid bed of balsam brush, while below her on the floor stood Rawhide, who received it and stowed it away under the bed, for what purpose was not apparent. Most of the damage being now done, I sat down and watched the exhibition with some interest until, it suddenly occurring to me that the blankets were missing, I interfered and found them tangled up with the brush under the bunk, and liberally salted with needles off the boughs.

At the height of the poaching season I received some information that caused me to pick up the beavers and keep them in the safety of the cabin for the matter of a week. They were now three parts grown and powerful for their size. The first night in camp they cut down a table, tore up part of the floor, upset a pail of water and broke a window, Their manner of accomplishing this last feat is worth recording. On the floor beside one wall was an eight foot canoe-pole with an iron socket on one end of it. I had noticed that they were fooling with this and had thought little of it, until they suddenly rushed the pole, heavy end foremost, across the floor together. When near the opposite wall Jelly Roll, who was ahead, reared up and held the end above her head with both hands, while Rawhide, at the other end, kept going and drove the iron socket crashing through the window. It is not to be supposed that they had any intention of deliberately breaking the glass, having no knowledge of its nature, their purpose being no doubt to commence the erection of a scaffold on which they could climb to close the aperture they thought existed there. But this notable instance is the only example that I have so far been a witness to, of actual team work on the part of beavers, in the carrying out of a plan of action conceived on the spur of the moment.

I wrote casual articles on all these doings, and the editor

who was taking my work wrote me that the interest aroused by these descriptions had prompted him to notify the National Parks Service of the Department of the Interior at Ottawa concerning them, with a view to having the beavers' activities placed on record in the form of moving pictures. Almost immediately I received a visit from an official of the National Parks Service, a gentleman with a wealth of iron grey hair, a shrewd but kindly face, and a pair of penetrating blue eyes that looked out at one, rather disconcertingly at times, from under his shaggy Scots eyebrows. At the railroad station he informed me that although he himself was convinced that my tale bore the stamp of authenticity, before any expensive operations could be undertaken, the lay-out would have to be looked over. He expressed himself as being prepared to see something a little unusual, but I will never quite forget the look on his face when, on arriving at the lake I called the beavers out, and swimming beneath the surface and unobserved by him, they suddenly popped out of the water beside him, climbed into the canoe, and gave him a very thorough examination. They mussed up his clothes but he cared little. The beavers were as represented, and that was that.

He stayed two days, and during that time the beavers were constantly in and out of the cabin. The beavers' actions had seemed very matter of fact to me, but this official told me frankly that there was nothing to parallel it anywhere, and that something must be done about it immediately before anything happened to the beavers. I told him the story of McGinnis and McGinty and how they had been the moving spirit behind this endeavour. He was quite moved by the recital and said that such a thing must not be allowed to happen again. However nothing was decided, save that when he left, he told me to expect a moving picture outfit to arrive within a few days.

In less than a week the cameras were grinding away while Jelly and Rawhide swam, dived, walked, ran, hauled sticks around, climbed in and out of a canoe, and did besides a hundred and one other things that no one had ever seen a beaver do before, and which formed the subject of the first beaver film of any account ever taken: 'The Beaver People'.

The difficulties connected with the filming of this first beaver picture were numerous. The operator who, in his enthusiasm, spent much of his time standing ankle deep in mud and water, and once slid waist deep into the creek, had little knowledge of beavers, and I had considerably less of picture taking, still or otherwise. The beavers were, however, very helpful, staying on deck all afternoon and acting very polite and interested, the main difficulty being to keep them far enough away from the cameras.

The picture was released and later in the year the official who had first approached me paid us another visit, and stated that he was now in a position to offer me the protection I so much desired for the beavers. The picture, he said, had been received with acclamation all over the Dominion, and was to be shown in all civilized countries. And you can bet we beaver people were a proud bunch.

It had been arranged that I might continue with the work I was now engaged in, under the auspices of the Dominion Government, and at a regular salary. The safety of the beavers would be guaranteed as long as they should live, and they would never be taken from me. Further, I would be given every opportunity to carry out my conservation ideas in a dignified and constructive manner, without the necessity for anxiety as to the means. A house would be built for Anahareo, to be designed according to our own plans. The beavers would be supplied with all the apples they could eat, and in return certain duties would be expected of them. They were to afford opportunities for research to students of wild life and natural history, and for scientific observation, and it was considered that the contribution they would make to a more general public knowledge of our national animal would constitute them a valuable educational exhibit of national importance and would provide a living argument for conservation. I myself would become a servant of the Government of Canada.

He skilfully drew me out, this earnest grey haired gentleman, and influenced by his utter friendliness and his attitude towards Indians, animals and all of nature, I told him of my ideas and aims, and of the bitter struggle it had been to keep on with them after such devastating failures. He listened in grave silence and when I had finished said, 'You're the man we want.' And from his further conversation I gathered that my activities had been under observation for some time past. And with his infinite tact and consideration he somehow made it appear that the gain would be his, that he was the petitioner, when my anxiety on behalf of my dependents must have been so very plain to see. But he did not hurry me, and went away leaving it in my hands to decide. And after I saw him off at the station, I went back behind the Elephant Mountain and thought it over.

It was the chance of a lifetime; yet the decision was a momentous one to make, and I gave the matter long and deep consideration.

Outside of forest ranging and guiding I had never had a job of any kind. If I embraced this opportunity, with all its multitudinous advantages, it would seem to mean the absolute surrendering of my freedom, might put an end to all my wanderings in the wilderness. It all seemed very final and a little frightening and unexpected. And two things stood out compellingly and clear as light: my object, which had seemed at last so unattainable, was now within my grasp, and my two small friends would be forever beyond the power of anyone to harm, free for all time from the haunting fear of death, that is the inescapable heritage of the beaver folk. These were the main issues; all others dwarfed beside them.

And so I chose aright for once, and today am freer than perhaps I ever was before, and have a little kingdom all my own.

And when I penned my letter of acceptance, turning over the beavers and myself to National Parks of Canada to do with as they would, I asked that we, the beavers and I, should never be parted, and that if I should ever find McGinnis and McGinty I would be allowed to take them too.

Both these requests were granted.

And thus I attained the consummation of my long thwarted desires and in a way I never dreamed of; not owing to any act of mine, but by reason of the vision and foresight of others. Long months, years of privation in pursuance of a principle, of futile tilting at lifeless and unimpressionable windmills, were bearing rather unexpected fruit. The tide of my affairs, that had ebbed so steadily, had turned to some effect. And none of it could have been made possible without the whole-hearted and vigorous, if unwitting, cooperation of two homely, clumsy looking, wilful and mischievous, yet lovable beasts.

Less than a week after the arrangements were concluded and I was to prepare myself to move, these contrary creatures suddenly absented themselves from me and all my works, and were, with no warning at all, frozen into their lodge for the winter.

They were now as far out of my reach as if they had been in China.

5

How we left Rawhide Lake

IT was a dreary winter. After the Beaver People had paid
me their last visit and danced for the last time their bizarre
Pleasure Dance upon the landing, and had retired to their
skilfully constructed hut at the head of lake, I found it
none too easy to adjust myself. The companionship of
these fun-loving, bustling little workers had become more
or less indispensable to me, and the knowledge that they
would spend the winter in comfort and security on the
fruits of a summer of intense industry, did little to lift the
pall of solitude that immediately fell upon the landscape.
The den that I had so carefully improved and lined with
marsh hay remained untenanted, and the big new tank,
especially made for them, sat in gloomy and resounding
emptiness in a corner. The constantly recurring thought
that my two retainers, now full grown and entirely beyond my influence, would revert to the wild state, and that
answering neither call nor entreaty would go sailing by on
the spring flood to the same fate that had befallen other
small adventurers, cast a gloom over the sunshiny days of
early winter.

Many were the pilgrimages made to the tall snow-
shrouded house at the far end of the lake, and often I carefully opened up the white coverlet and spoke through the
hollow air-space beneath it, the well-known words and
phrases that so far had never failed to provoke weird contortions and sounds of joy. But now no sound rewarded

me save the echo of my own voice across the empty solitude. Yet beneath that conical white mound that stood high above the level of the wind-swept muskeg was life, and two plump furry bodies lay sleeping soundly, little knowing that the very defences on which they so depended served but to advertise their presence to every passing vandal. Well I knew that did I betray my trust and neglect to guard these living creatures committed to my charge, they would never see the spring.

The small receiving set had now become an important factor in my life, for here was an inexhaustible supply of company and music on tap, and I went to much trouble to keep the batteries replenished, drawing them in and out on the sleigh at frequent intervals.

When Christmas came I went out, but my heart was not in the festivities of the generous family that had me for a guest, so I spent New Year's at the cabin, listening to the celebrations on the radio. I had by now got into the way of keeping these festivals in some kind of a way, and at midnight, aroused by the announcements that came to me from out this blind man's theatre, and stirred by the knowledge that the whole world was enjoying itself, I did not see why Rawhide Lake should be left out of it. So I turned on the electric torch and let it stream through the window, down on to the frozen lake, and in the spotlight of its beam I stood at the water hole and fired a few shots in the air, and yelled a little. And I fired one shot straight and true to the eastward, towards the far off House of McGinnis and its helpful happy ghosts, and another over the north, towards Chibougamou, where my prospector was. And on each bullet I breathed a message, and sent it out into the vast emptiness of the New Year's night.

Meanwhile, between patrols, I wandered through the uplands and followed the old disused lumber roads to see what lay at the end of them; but it was like wandering through an empty haunted house. There was never anything but an old deserted camp surrounded by stumps and stark dead trees, ghosts of a forest that was gone. There were small blocks of timber, and here and there a lone pine tree, diseased perhaps and spared on that account. I always made my dinner fire near one of these and tried to feel at home. But it was beyond my imagination; they were destined for the axe in any case and I could only pity them. And on leaving I would look back a dozen times at the moving smoke of my lunch fire, as though it were something there that was alive and kept the old tree company when I was gone.

All Northern people loved the pine trees, perhaps because those of us of any age at all had lived the forepart of our lives among them. Now, as we followed the receding waves of this vanishing frontier further and further North to where pine no longer grew, we found them to be rare, and missed them. There were not even any wolves here, and a country without them seemed lacking in some strong ingredient. I missed their wild cantatas, and the lazy inbred deer, lacking any incentive to move around and improve themselves, died like rabbits all through the woods.

In town I met one Indian. Civilization had surely got in its work on him. He had a broad Cockney accent, and a large repertoire of shanty songs which he rendered most entertainingly. He was more or less of a hobo and was well versed in his art. He could size up a store full of people and pick his prospect unerringly, extracting from him a nickel, a dime, or a quarter, or whatever he appeared to be good for, before the astonished victim quite realized what it was all about. He was a great thief, so he told me with some pride, but as he was on his uppers and his company might be entertaining, I had him stay with me a while. He practised none of his accomplishments on me, and was a good worker around the place, and weaved some very fine baskets from strips he skilfully pounded out of ash timber, and dyed. But he was afflicted with what he termed 'itchy feet', a malady which could only be alleviated by the soothing contact of long stretches of railroad ties, applied at regular intervals. So one morning, with one of his small baskets filled with supplies he set out, bound for no particular place, singing happily as he went, a piece of drift flung from the spinning flywheel of Modernity, a shred of waste material spewed from the bowels of the machine that would some day engulf us all. And as he disappeared, this cheerful vagabond, amongst the trees along the outbound trail, his song echoing back behind him, I remembered that he belonged to the oldest civilized of all the tribes. The wild freedom of his ancestors that had made them something noble, perverted, was come to this.

No son should ever be mine to rear to such a heritage.

And then one day I returned from patrol to find sitting in the cabin waiting for me, Anahareo! She had come out to civilization by plane. We had much to talk about, and we talked about it – plenty. Although she was prepared, by my few letters, to hear that my attempts to recover McGinnis and McGinty had been unsuccessful, when I told her that there had been no trace of them, no sign, nothing – and when, to prove to her how thorough had been the search, I described the history of the past year and a half, and told her straight that there could be no longer any hope, she did not trust herself to speak, just held the relics in her hand and looked at them. And she stayed so for a long time, turning the dry, dead keepsakes over and over on their buckskin wrapper, and at last said softly, 'Don't let's ever forget, will we, eh? Never?'

Her greatest wish could now never be accomplished, and save at Christmas, in commemoration of that one unforgettable Christmas Eve on faraway Birch Lake, she never mentions our little old companions that are gone.

As to her own affairs, her tale was quickly told. The Depression, so soon to make itself felt the world over, was already on its way. The mining business had not been what it was cracked up to be; her claims, any claims in fact, were unsaleable, and had become something in the nature of a whole herd of white elephants. They were eating up money faster than she could earn it, so she had relinquished them, and had got out of the country while she still had the price to do so. But her joy at all the good news I had for her made these matters of small moment, in her estimation. She had had what she called her 'fling' and was satisfied. But there was a note of sadness in her triumph when she spoke of Dave. Some busy-body, full of ideas of uplift and education of the savage mind, had painstakingly explained to him that his long cherished belief that somewhere beyond the northern horizon there existed a vast unexplored hunting ground, was a delusion; that the white people had penetrated to the furthermost recesses of the wilderness, and that the end had been reached, that there were no more beavers, no more pine trees; it was all a myth. Dave had only half believed in those things; but this stark and utter disillusionment, together with the loss of his fortune so nearly won, had ruthlessly tumbled his house of cards about his ears. His dream shattered, his last hope gone, he had brooded and fallen into a melancholy from which he could not be aroused; his age had come upon him all at once, and left him a weary, unhappy old man.

And one night, not long before the falling of the leaves, he had come to bid Anahareo good-bye. He was going home. And with his canoe – my last gift to him – his beloved gun, and his recollections, he had paddled away into the calm moonlight night, on his way back to the scenes of his childhood, broken, hopeless, and alone.

The winter was not without event. The book was accepted, and it had been published practically verbatim. The results were numerous and interesting. Small amounts began to percolate into the bank. The workings of a bank account were, and are yet, a puzzle to me, and although these amounts were quite small and continue to remain so, I found writing cheques on the brilliantly printed slips provided an exciting and adventurous pastime. We both got a great kick out of having the people at the other end accept them. Moreover there was the delightfully informal correspondence entered into on occasions when the sums indicated on these gay coloured tokens were in excess of the funds. I have since, however, succeeded in working out a system whereby I can forecast this contingency quite accurately.

My writings began to appear in different publications. Some editors, and kindly, wished to make changes in my work, substituting for my faulty phrasing, constructions more in accordance with correct usage. But these alterations seemed somehow to destroy the effect I attempted to produce, and unable to adjust myself to the higher standards so set up, I objected strenuously. After some lively discussions back and forth, my requests were acceded to, probably more to put an end to the correspondence than anything else. Editors, it seems, can be not such bad fellows after all.

I received numbers of press notices. Most reviewers, realizing perhaps my lack of technical knowledge, were kind and let me down easy, even praised me. Some of them encouraged me to try again, and in some American and

English newspapers my work was given several columns of favourable comment. Letters came from Germany, Australia, London and New York; a Canadian college in Ontario – my home Province – gave it recognition. I felt elated, yet somehow apprehensive – I had started something; I had fired an arrow, wildly, in the air and it had come home to roost, and in great feather. One or two critics, mildly scandalized apparently that an uncultured bushwhacker of acknowledged native blood should so step out of character and become articulate, were more severe. They seemed to take it as a personal affront that there were in existence beings who, without benefit of education, had common knowledge of many things not taught in halls of learning, casting, by implication, some doubt on my knowledge of a subject with which they themselves could have had but little acquaintance. They probably did not realize that the rather standardizing influence of an intensive education militates somewhat against the development of an ability to grasp the more subtle and elusive nuances of a culture peculiar to the wilderness.

There were other developments; my mail increased to alarming proportions. The world, I found, had a number of very wonderful people in it, and some of these letters made me feel that I was at last emerging from the role of despoiler and had joined, even if in a very minor capacity, the ranks of the producers. These acknowledgements of appreciation made us both very happy. It was not now so much like shouting blindly out into the darkness. Our aims were actually considered sane and reasonable.

Interviewers appeared who put us gently through our paces. We were invited to a convention in Montreal; I was supposed to speak. Having, with great difficulty, though with no great certainty, persuaded Anahareo that she would not be called on, I finally persuaded her to accept her end of the invitation, and come along to supply the well known moral support. We arranged for a couple of friends to undertake the beaver patrol and went down together. The train drew into the city by some back entrance or other, and the portentous and over-powering gloom of huge industrial buildings just about had me buffaloed, as I realized that this appalling pile of stone and iron was the city that I was to electrify with my remarks. However, as with a war-bonnet, the front view of it was better than the back, and Mr Dallyn, the editor who had done so much for us and who was now our host, was seated in the audience with Anahareo, and as he had suggested, I addressed my speech to them, the rest listening in at their own risk. Here we saw the beaver picture for the first time.

From now on I met and conferred with many conservationists, professed and real. The genuine conservationist was unmistakeable, and I made a number of worthwhile and highly instructive contacts, not a few of which still continue. But some of these gentlemen, while enthusiastic, were faintly ridiculous in their insistence on getting full credit for every word said or written by them for their cause, while we could not see that it mattered a great deal who said or wrote what, so long as we got results.

There was a rather depressing suspicion that others were interested in no measures in which the subdued rustle of currency was not somewhere audible; and there is a melancholy fear that the left hands of a good many of these gentlemen were well advised of what their right hand was about to do, a couple of good jumps in advance. But by far the greatest part of my contacts were with sincere and earnest men who had the situation with regard to wild life very much to heart, and I formed many associations that were an inspiration and that formed the basis of more than one friendship.

With regard to an issue so new and having as yet no definite policy, arguments were inevitable. Some thought that all remaining timber should be turned over to commercial interest, the practice of reforestation being their platform. I gave as my views that reforestation, while it should be carried on intensively was not preservation but substitution, and that in face of the fact that it took a hundred years to grow a respectable tree, its undue propagation as a sole means of restitution, amounted to an attempt to run a bill with the nation which would not be payable for a century or so, by which time, it seemed to me, the debtors would be safely out of it, and would care little who was to foot the bill. These kitchen garden forests, I urged, while as necessary to the development of the country as were fields of grain, could never replace the magnificent forests of great trees that they supplanted, citing, in support of my contention, the notorious example of Green Timbers on the Pacific Highway. Others thought that fur farming solved the wild life problem, which I was persuaded it never could do, save commercially, and added a statement I had heard on the radio, to the effect that the value of wild life as a tourist attraction in the United States, was worth some hundreds of millions of dollars yearly, asking my opponents what they thought of that for a commercial enterprise. It was all a matter of opinion and these discussions were very stimulating, and enabled me to grasp other points of view besides my own.

I had offers, highly remunerative some of them, but none that could afford the beavers the same protection that National Parks had guaranteed.

Meanwhile, in advices received from Ottawa, we learned that Jelly and her leading man had attracted wide attention, not only at home, but overseas and across the border, of which they were supremely unconscious as they lay snoring together in their castle of frozen mud.

In March we commenced our campaign for their recovery, for we had no idea what would be their attitude towards us after five months spent in seclusion and entirely beyond our influence. We commenced by cutting a hole in the ice near the feed raft, and found it to have been nearly consumed, and this we replaced at intervals with fresh birch, poplar, and willow, which was always taken away piecemeal, though we never saw a beaver.

April came and with it warm days, melting snows and shaky ice. It now became necessary, if possible, to reestablish communication with our long absent friends. Being now two years old, and having been completely out of contact with human beings for five and a half months, and at a phase in their lives during which they usually desert their own home and parents and branch out to establish for themselves, their spirit of independence might be stronger than memory or affection. My experience with beavers, although wide and life-long, had not hitherto included any such situation as now presented itself. Nonetheless I designed and filled in the specifications for transportation tanks and boxes, and carried on my preparations for the removal with all confidence.

We transported our entire equipment, save a few necessaries, to the railroad ready for shipment, and gave away all but a little of our remaining provisions. Having now burnt our bridges behind us, we went to work. We cut two holes in the ice opposite the lodge and placed in them a choice assortment of poplar and willow, already budding and succulent with sap commencing to rise in the early spring sun. This provision was persistently destroyed by the constant nibbling of the hungry muskrats, whom we frequently saw, and we as regularly replaced it.

At these holes we watched, turn about, from sunset till

daylight, and one evening after about a week of this, during my turn of duty at this listening post, I saw the swirl and larger bubbles of the passage there of a beaver, and noted that although he eventually took away a stick, he passed around the hole several times, far enough back to be out of sight, apparently searching systematically for one that might protrude beyond the open water, in under the ice. I set the next bait further into the centre of the hole so as to be in plain view, but nothing was then taken till after dark. The reason for these manoeuvres was, I believe, the extreme sensitiveness of the eyes to light after a long period spent in the darkness and much sleeping.

The weather turned soft and the ice began to give out along the shore line, and we took turns or sat hours together motionless, a little distance from the holes, calling softly with the inflections that had in the past always elicited a response, until on the third evening, after a preliminary and very lengthy inspection from under a hollow shelf of ice, a beaver broke water, emitted a long low call and disappeared with a mighty splurge. After perhaps half an hour, during which we sat tensely waiting, calling at intervals, the beaver reappeared, swam uncertainly around for a few minutes, and being at last satisfied with our appearance, climbed out on the ice beside us and commenced the well-known and oft-repeated toilet – Jelly Roll, the Boss, in person: the same voice, the same clumsy waddle, and the same air of arrogant self-sufficiency as she took an apple, and shaking it back and forth with little squeals, ate it with evident enjoyment within reach of our hand.

Triumph! After nearly six months in the wild state she had returned to us, faithful as the seasons themselves. But I was dubious about my little wild fellow, who had stayed with me unasked and of his own accord, and whose gentle trusting ways had made his short stay with me so pleasant.

However we continued calling over two more nights, and once by the light of the young moon saw a dark object lying motionless on the water in the most distant of the holes. Jelly was beside us, fussing around our feet, and the shape of the floating object was unmistakably that of another beaver. That he was very much alive was evidenced by his abrupt disappearance at some movement. The next night he took an apple with every sign of confidence, and the following evening spent a considerable time out on the ice in company with the Boss and ourselves.

Again triumph; a wild beaver tamed by hand but never captive, he had come back to us from his natural state after nearly half a year of absence. Almost unbelievable it seemed, but there he was and not to be denied. The atmosphere brightened considerably after this, and I had no further doubt as to the outcome.

I went out to town and wired the National Parks Service that the beavers had surrendered themselves.

Now to capture them, remove them from a home to which they must have become attached, and to inflict on them the terrifying alarms and hardships of a journey of a thousand miles or more, without impairing this wonderful confidence and fidelity in the simple mind of a wild animal. You have but to fool them once or twice and the work of years becomes null and void; and only by the most delicate tact and diplomacy can the lost ground be recovered, if at all, especially with the more intelligent species.

I attempted to secure Jelly Roll the following evening, but she had so increased in size and strength that I found it impossible to lift her from the ground without a struggle, the very thing I wished to avoid. We both tried it without success; we could pull her ears, open her mouth, yank her tail and roll her on her back, do anything in fact that we pleased, but this lifting business was now strictly against the rules. So a wooden box was constructed and laid on its back, with the lid lying flat and facing the water, and into this, all unsuspicious, walked the Boss. With the guilty feelings of those who betray a friend, even if only for his own good, we promptly stood up the box and clapped down the lid. Swiftly adjusting the tump-line we were quickly away with our load. Voiceless, motionless, the Boss stood the gaff until liberated in the camp, when the first dumb bewilderment gave way to wild clutchings and wailings as she seized hold of parts of my apparel. Her fright was quite pathetic, and she had to be pacified and reassured almost as much as a child would have been, and nothing would now do her but that I should pick her up like the big tub she was, while she buried her head in my clothing. Gradually she commenced to look around, and finding herself in familiar surroundings eventually recovered her composure.

Rawhide was a good deal harder to capture as he would not enter the box, and on this particular night had decided not to leave the water. But I eventually got my hands on him and he submitted quite docilely to being carried away, and was a good deal easier to handle than Jelly had been. The beavers made no attempt to escape during the night and slept soundly with us in the blankets, and the next morning they submitted quietly to being placed in a ventilated tin box provided for the purpose, and all hands hit the trail for town.

We said good-bye to the empty cabin and the now deserted lake that had been our home for almost two years, and we were not a little lonesome as we trudged over the snowshoe trail, drawing our living freight behind us, leaving behind us forever, somewhere, those that I had stayed here so long to seek. My search, carried on hopelessly for two years, was over.

The Quebec Government had waived all rights in any of our pets, and the permit, as promised, called for four beavers. But in the big tank so carefully designed, there were two extra places that were empty.

A deputation of citizens came to see us off and we left real friends behind us in that town. And as the train pulled out at last, we stood hand in hand on the step of the hindmost car, never moving, never speaking, watching Temiscouata and its mountains slowly fade from view.

6

How the Pilgrimage was ended

It is now Fall, the time of Harvest, and the Queen and her little band are busy gathering in supplies against the long Winter, as are the more responsible and useful members of society everywhere.

Landings have been reopened and runways cleaned out, and into them with uncanny accuracy trees fall crashing at almost any hour from four in the afternoon till daylight. The feed raft that floats before the cabin[1] is getting daily heavier, wider, and more solid. Heavy logs are piled on it to sink it deeper, while on the underside the limbs and branches of the fallen trees and all the choicest portions,

1. These beavers are so attached to their human associates that they have taken advantage of a tunnel that was bored for their convenience when the cabin was built, and have constructed over the mouth of it, inside the residence, a large beaver house which occupies nearly one third of the floor space, is about twelve feet across, and would weigh not less than a ton. The beavers bring the building materials in through the door, which they are able to open from either side, and the entire family uses this erection as a permanent abode, summer and winter. From it they have egress into deep water through the tunnel, and they attach their feed raft to the front of the cabin, which abuts onto the lake. Having successfully adjusted their arrangements to suit these unusual conditions, they live and carry on their normal activities precisely as do their wild brethren. The adults have never been known to leave the body of water on which they are domiciled, though no restraint has ever been placed on their movements. The young, on attaining maturity, follow their natural course and spread out through the surrounding lakes and streams to mingle with the native beavers, and are frequently seen.

many of them with a short projection used as a retaining hook, are secured below the reach of ice.

Heavily laden beavers swim slowly by separately, in groups, or all in line as on parade, their loads gaily caparisoned with sprays of coloured leaves like trappings – the Pageant of the Workers of the Wild. Sometimes I tune in on some symphonic orchestra, and they go sailing by in their steady slow procession to the martial strains of Zampa or the Polonaise, or slip silently along the shadowy surface of the water while the Moonlight Sonata weaves a spell about them – pictures in sound I wish that half the world were here to see.

At this season young beavers commence to perform some useful work, but up to this time few of the rules which govern adult beaver behaviour seem to apply to the kittens. They lead a happy carefree existence of playing, wrestling, and exploring. They roam the waters of the home-pond in pairs or groups, forming attachments among themselves, signalling with shrill cries when separated. They pester the older beavers at their work, and although this must be very exasperating, the adults show no sign of irritation, and will go to a great deal of trouble to avoid injuring them accidently. This is difficult as the little fellows seem to be always in the way of a heavy log or under a pile of limbs, or crowded together at the foot of a runway. They seem to be protected by the good luck that favours irresponsibles, and come out of every jam unhurt and looking for more excitement.

The passage near any group of them of a large beaver with a tow, is a heavensent opportunity for excitement. With a concerted rush they attack the convoy, attaching themselves to the load, pulling at it, cutting pieces off it, climbing on the laden animal's back, or vainly trying to engage him in a wrestling match or some other aquatic sport. Such diversions serve to break the monotony of life on a small pond, but are a serious matter for the harassed object of this persecution, who takes it all in good part. The adults are not above resorting to such subterfuges as waiting motionless until the band of marauders disperses, or diving suddenly with the tow and swimming beneath the surface to dislodge them from it; but these stratagems seldom succeed, as at the first movement, or in the latter case on their reappearance from the depths, the parasitic little demons descend upon them, and pursue them until they have disposed of their load. As the season advances these corsairs cease their piratical activities, and direct their abounding energies into more productive channels, and can be seen hauling in their own small loads regularly and with great diligence.

Most all day a complete and utter silence reigns upon the pond. But about an hour before sundown, first one then another black head breaks water, loud cries and signals echo back and forth, and soon the hitherto calm water and the deserted lake shore near the cabin becomes a scene of activity reminiscent of that to be seen around the old red school house at four o'clock.

It would seem that the task of identifying each and every beaver, all so similar in appearance, were well nigh impossible. It can, however, be done. Before two months of age they stick pretty closely to the house, during which period I put in my more intensive training operations; after that time they develop individual characteristics of voice and action, or slight variations in shape which, if studied closely, make them recognizable. They seem to run in types, each brood exhibiting distinct personalities similar to those of the last one; so that there is always the Loud Talker, the Independent, the Mad Hatter, the Busy Appearing One, or the Lazy Bones, or the One That Stays

Out Late. Before I got on to this I used to count as high as twenty beavers, as alike as peas or houseflies, when there were only four or six. Fortunately, although they are constantly on the move, they go in groups of two or three together, and there being only a limited number of them, I do not have to be in more than two or three widely separated places at the one time, in order to count heads before they switch places and intermingle.

We used to name all the new arrivals as soon as they began to be distinguishable, so we had Happy and Hooligan, Wakinee and Wakinoo, Silver Heels and Buckshot, Sugar Loaf and Jelly Roll Number Two, and a host of others, but eventually we ran out of names. They never answered to them anyway, but would always come to one particular call, a plaintive wailing note pitched in a close resemblance to a common signal of their own, though different enough for them to recognize its origin. This cry was a prolonged, 'Mah—W–e–e–e–e–e,' given with a wavering inflexion, and its sound, repeated a few times, rarely failed to attract one or other of them, or at least elicit an answering hail. It became at last, by long usage, a kind of community name for them, and we came to call them, each and every one Mah-Wee; so if one was called they all came, a very convenient arrangement. This name was very suitable in more ways than one, as it is similar in sound to the Ojibway word signifying 'to cry,' a vocal expedient they made use of on the slightest pretext. Such, however, is their independence of character that once having put in an appearance, or given some more or less heedful answer to the summons, it would be some hours before they would again respond to it. They could, however, be depended on to appear at least three times a night and also for the usual morning check up when they returned to retire for the day.

The depredations continue as of yore. Often I enter the cabin after some lengthy absence on patrol to find my quarters have been invaded, and almost invariably some burglary has been committed. Perhaps a lot of potatoes has had the lid picked neatly off and every potato taken out of it. Once these potatoes were in a stew and had had to be fished for. A beaver's hands are not made for fishing, but this difficulty was easily overcome by upsetting the stew-pot, with more or less gratifying results. Sometimes the woodbox has been emptied, a box of apples opened, or a chair hauled down into the lake, and being useless for any purpose, abandoned there. Dishes, apparently, are trophies of high value; unless fastened down, their rice dish is removed as soon as it is empty and is never seen again. Several have been lost that way, though one of them was, after three months, very politely returned one evening and was found, high and dry and very clean, up on the bank beside the house.

I returned from a perhaps too lengthy visit to a neighbouring Ranger's camp, and on going behind the cabin to collect some wood I had split for the night, found it to be all gone; also, some green poles collected for fuel were not to be seen. The interest aroused by these features prevented me from noting further and far more interesting developments till, finding the place kind of bare, I suddenly missed the store tent. Investigation revealed that it was down, and that most of the poles that had held it up had disappeared. Fortunately it had been empty. The stationary saw-horse, being made of green poplar, had been cut off close to the ground and spirited away bodily and never was seen again. This, of course, was the work of the Queen, levying taxes on the estate. There was nothing so unusual about this, except that it had been the only time that I had ever permitted myself to overstay.

I receive numbers of communications in regard to conservation and kindred subjects, and I have several bags filled with them, sorted into lots. Wishing once to look through one of these bags, I brought it into the camp and thoughtlessly left it standing in a corner. Being busy outside, I paid it no further attention for the time being until, looking for the letters, I found them gone, bag and all. A disturbance in the beaver house, which I had been wondering about in a detached sort of way, indicated that the booty had been brought in and was being forcibly divided. Screams and squeals of outrage in a well known voice apprised me of the identity of the thief, as Jelly struggled against hopeless odds to maintain her rights. The resultant uproar was little short of appalling, and the scene must have been ludicrous in the extreme as she tussled valiantly and vainly for the possession of her prize which, consisting of some hundreds of letters, was entirely beyond her control.

Perhaps she thought that having been for a long time now a Star of no mean magnitude, it was about time she had some fan mail of her own. Anyway that mail remains unanswered to this day but, as it was all used for bedding for the entire beaver family, it was utilized in a way that the writers never imagined in their wildest dreams. So these epistles are serving the purpose of conservation after all, which is what they were originally intended to do in any case.

While the ice is making, the beavers succeed in keeping open a channel to their accessible cuttings, in which they tow supplies up to the last minute. The whole family breaks ice for several hours each day to accomplish this, succeeding in keeping it open for perhaps a week, but this watery highway eventually freezes over. Jelly then takes to frequenting the water hole, after one has been opened for our own purposes, and through it, I give her quantities of apples, sometimes till nearly Christmas. She takes them all away, by relays, and on her return home the sounds of strife, followed by a steady and contented munching mingled with grunts of satisfaction in different keys, give evidence of her generosity to those who make up in appetite what they lack in enterprise.

I surmise that air that is very frosty must cause discomfort to lungs acclimatized to soft weather and the humid atmosphere of a beaver house. I was led to believe this by the fact that in cold weather she never emitted any of her usual sounds of greeting when her head appeared, and closer inspection showed that on cold nights she never drew breath while in the open, which accounted for her hurried withdrawals. I now allow a scum of ice to form, and shove the apples under it. So I do not see her, but the apples disappear with monotonous regularity, until the arrival of more severe weather makes this practice inadvisable.

About a year and a half ago another subject was added to Jelly's fast spreading kingdom. A little daughter came to us. She and the Queen get along well together, but we do not leave her in accessible places, as Jelly's habit of appropriating articles which she takes a fancy to, might result in us having to open the beaver house and rescue a very wet and outraged young woman from the ministrations of her triumphant abductor.

Although Jelly is by about ten pounds the heavier, they are much of a size, and stand boldly up to one another and sometimes talk together. And as neither one of them can, as yet, speak any English, a conversation is held the like of which has not, I think, ever been heard before. The little girl is delighted when this big, dark furry toy, this good natured teddy-bear with the so pretty coloured teeth[1] takes an apple from her hand. Gently the beaver takes the offer-

1. The incisor teeth of a mature beaver are a dark orange in colour.

ing, with none of the tom-boy gambols she indulges in with us, and yet never so gently as Rawhide, humble, tireless, patient Rawhide, changeless and unchangeable as the courses of the Wilderness whose son he is. He never seems to mind his crippled foot that looks so odd beside the good one. He has his work, his babies that he loves so unselfishly and, in his simple way he is happy. Sometimes, as he sits regarding me so attentively and so inscrutably, I would give much to know what deliberations are going on behind that impassive mask, back of those grave, observing eyes.

For he is the silent power behind the Throne at Beaver Lodge, and should he some day decide to move his people away from here, no power on earth short of confinement or death could ever stop him. So it behoves me well that I should not offend.

He and Jelly are known, in some small way, in many countries, but they sleep on in unconscious innocence of their celebrity. And as they lie there snoring in contentment, I wonder if the Queen remembers the dingy camp in far off Temiscouata, the bed, the table, the deerskin rugs on which she used to sleep before the stove, the welcomes home she used to have for me. Or if she has ever a passing thought for the long lonely days before the coming of Rawhide, when we were such good company and often slept together, and how she used to 'help' me get water, and would shut the door in my face; and how we wrote our book, and how she got lost and must have nearly died – and how Anahareo came back to us again.

Perhaps these matters are only a dim recollection now, and meanwhile she lords it over Rawhide and Anahareo and little Dawn and all the rest of us, and is content.

Epilogue

It is now the Moon of Snowshoes. Anahareo and the small new daughter are spending the Winter out in town. The beavers are safely stowed away within their fortress. The visits and the begging and the frolics, the apple raids, the shoutings and the stealing are all over for the time, laid away securely for the Winter. And I am lonesome for them all, and so I spend my time with them on paper.

And as I pen some dry precise report, in which I weigh my words and balance supposition with proven fact, I feel that I am giving all the best I have to this labour that has fallen to my lot – that I am keeping faith.

And I know, too, that my work which I had thought had reached its consummation, has only now begun.

Out on the frozen frontage of my cabin stands another lodge, a replica of the one indoors. It is at present empty. No doubt it will be put to some use, according to some plan the owners have, of which I anxiously await the fulfilment. This house-to-let is a pretty bleak and lonesome looking erection, and at times I feel rebuffed as I look at it in the pale glow of the Northern lights.

But on entering the cabin and hailing the invisible company who occupy the lodge that stands within it, I get a lazy mumbled answer to my call. I hear also a few whimpers of protest from bedfellows who enter sleepily into the age-old discussion as to who has all the bed.

Sounds of slumber issue from the bowels of the thick-walled lodge, as some tired worker rolls over on his back and snores prodigiously in the security he has worked so hard to earn, while he dreams, perhaps, of rows of shining poplar trees, of new, undiscovered streams, or of lake shores lined with apples.

And I know that all is well with my little company of fellow pilgrims, and that I also may now call it the end of a day.

And here they will always be, in the peace and quietness of their silent lake amongst the hills, till they pass on in the fullness of time to join the hosts of their brethren who have gone before them, leaving behind them others in their stead who may perpetuate, in each their turn and for all time to come, the ancient and honourable traditions of the Beaver People.

On all sides from the cabin where I write extends an un-interrupted wilderness, flowing onwards in a dark billowing flood Northward to the Arctic Sea. No railroad passes through it to burn and destroy, no settler lays waste with fire and axe. Here from any eminence a man may gaze on unnumbered leagues of forest that will never feed the hungry maw of commerce.

This is a different place, a different day.

Nowhere does the sight of stumps and slashed tops of noble trees offend the eye or depress the soul, and the strange, wild, unimaginable beauty of these Northern sunsets is not defaced by jagged rows of stark and' ghastly rampikes.

The camp is known as Beaver Lodge; yet to us it will always be a replica of that House, the Empty Cabin, that is so far away – a little richer perhaps, a little better built, but the spirit is the same. Save for the radio, the kitchen range, the shape of the roof, it is as near to it as maybe. It is built of logs; the windows face out on the groves of trees. A painted warrior stands post in his appointed place, his eagle bonnet spread in brave array; the paint work, the emblems, they have all been reproduced. The tokens are all here.

Atavistic? Perhaps it is; but good has come of it.

Every wish has been fulfilled, and more. Gone is the haunting fear of a vandal hand. Wild life in all its rich variety, creatures deemed furtive and elusive, now pass almost within our reach, and sometimes stand beside the camp and watch. And birds, and little beasts and big ones, and things both great and small have gathered round the place, and frequent it, and come and go their courses as they will, and fly or swim or walk or run according to their kind.

Death falls, as at times it must, and Life springs in its place. Nature lives and journeys on and passes all about in well balanced, orderly array.

The scars of ancient fires are slowly healing over; big trees are growing larger. The beaver towns are filling up again.

The cycle goes on.

The Pilgrimage is over.

Some Other Puffins You Might Enjoy

BREAK FOR FREEDOM
Ewan Clarkson

Syla was a mink, and so dark brown she looked almost black.

The cage where she lived was identical with all the others, except for one thing – there was a loose staple in the floor of her sleeping box. And that was the way that Syla escaped from the fur farm to find a new life, free in a remote valley on the edge of Dartmoor, free to hunt and fish and play, and also to face the dangers of traps or sudden chills or fierce animals.

Ewan Clarkson is an expert naturalist and makes a fascinating story of Syla's year on the moor, her brief courtship with another escaped mink and her life with her cubs. At the same time he tells us about all the other inhabitants of Dartmoor, the birds and insects, snakes and rodents, till the moor seems as busy and complicated as the greatest human city.

For readers of eleven upwards.

THE CUSTER WOLF
Roger Caras

One April five wolf cubs were born in a cave under a tree stump. One was white, and men would come to call him by a name that would live in history, for this was the beginning of the legend of the Custer Wolf.

This wolf inexplicably grew up different from any other. He was a beautiful but solitary animal and as he grew it became clear that he killed for the love of killing and terrorized a huge area round the town of Custer for six whole years.

Sometimes he killed thirty cattle in a week, more than he could possibly eat, and he took incredible chances, yet he escaped every trap that was set and every gun that was fired. Small wonder that the men believed the white wolf was charmed.

GREYFRIARS BOBBY
Eleanor Atkinson

The best thing about the story of *Greyfriars Bobby* is that it is absolutely true. There really *was* a little dog in Edinburgh called Bobby: he was a Skye Terrier, and he loved his master, a shepherd called Auld Jock, very dearly. When Auld Jock died Bobby would not leave his grave in Greyfriars Churchyard. People tried to take the little dog away, and found him a home in the country, but still he came back and lived in the church-yard where his friends brought him food. He died after fourteen years and was so famous that a fountain with his statue on it was put up in his memory.

The book includes illustrations taken from Walt Disney's film about him.

TARKA THE OTTER
Henry Williamson

This story of an otter is as true as long observations and keen insight could make it. It lets you live with Tarka and see at his level (much closer to the ground than our eye level) the wild life of that stretch of Devon country which runs from Dartmouth to the sea, between the rivers Torridge and Taw. With a good map you can follow almost every step of the story.

To read *Tarka* for the first time is a tremendous experience whatever your age. It would be a pity to try it too young, but most people over ten will enjoy it.